THE AX,
THE ROOT
AND THE
WITHERED FRUIT

PASTOR KEN REED

ISBN 978-1-0980-4442-8 (paperback)
ISBN 978-1-0980-4443-5 (hardcover)
ISBN 978-1-0980-4444-2 (digital)

Christian Faith Publishing, Inc.
832 Park Avenue
Meadville, PA 16335
www.christianfaithpublishing.com

Printed in the United States of America

For anyone who has responded to Jesus as Savior and Redeemer, there is no more authoritative understanding than this, God and His Word is true; this is the foundation for every believer's faith.

> For what if some did not believe? Will their unbelief make the faithfulness of God without effect? Certainly not! Indeed, let God be true but every man a liar. (**Romans 3:3–4a**)

> God is not a man, that he should lie, nor a son of man, that he should change his mind. Does he speak and then not act? Or does he promise and not fulfill? (**Numbers 23:19**)

For the Purpose
of Our Study

I'm defining truth in this three-part construct

First truth is focused on—scripture when conveying God's will and purpose for Jesus.

Second truth is focused on—the power of the Holy Spirit active within this purpose.

Third truth is focused on—understanding our necessity for mixing faith in God's process.

Key

===

As we continually apply this process in faith, no weapon that sets itself against us can prosper. It is possible for you and me to consistently experience God's kingdom, as being present and active in us, i.e.—God's kingdom and will being done on earth just as in heaven.

A Focus on the Things that Are True

Only God's truth sets and keeps us free—truth is God's delivery system for the continual release of His people from our constant exposure to deceit, darkness, and deception.

Key

==

> Truth is what God said, not what we think He said, truth is what God means, not what we think He means.

> For my thoughts are not your thoughts,
> neither are my ways, your ways, saith the Lord.
> **(Isaiah 55: 8)**

With that being said, what we think about and the way we think about them become critical. Therefore, our thinking can keep us imprisoned either as a slave to sin or as one who's fully released, i.e., "free indeed," just as God intended through Jesus Christ.

> As a man thinks in his heart so is, he.
> **(Proverbs 27:3)**

> The eye is the lamp of the body. If your eyes are good, your whole body will be full of light. But if your eyes are bad, your whole body will be full of darkness. If then, the light within you is darkness, how great is that darkness! No one can serve two masters, either he will hate the one and love the other, or he will be devoted to the one, and despise the other, you cannot serve both God and mammon. **(Matthew 6: 22–25)**

I'm aware of the context and focus of this verse especially its implication regarding material things, "no one can serve two masters." But there is a Kingdom Principle revealed here as well, one which has practical application. Our willingness to embrace this principle determines its capacity to fully impact us.

If the things we focus on are true, i.e., "full of light" then, our whole life experience is a progression of freedom and release.

But if the things we focus on are not true, i.e., "full of darkness," then our lives are littered with deceptions and entanglements and having legal authority to hold us in places of struggle and captivity.

God's Creative Order Restored

From the end of the sixth day of creation, mankind, i.e., (Adam) was created "in the image and likeness of God."

> And God said let us make man in our image,
> and in our likeness. **(Gen. 1:26)**

However, after the fall; a startling transformation occurs, in that all of mankind, is now being birthed and, now in the image and likeness of Adam I.e. fallen man.

Genesis 5:1–3 This is the book of the genealogy of Adam, "In the day that God created man, he made him in the likeness of God. He created them male and female and blessed them and called them mankind in the day they were created. And Adam lived 130 years, and begot a son in his own likeness, after his image, and named him Seth."

But now, in Christ Jesus, you and I have become a brand-new creation, i.e., a never before existing species of being.

> Therefore if any man be in Christ Jesus, he is a new creation, the old things have passed away, and all things have become new. **(2 Corinthians 5:17)**

However, through the Redemptive work of Jesus on the Cross; God, has restored fallen man i.e. (you and me) back into His own image and likeness.

As he is so are, we in this world.
(1 John 4: 17)

We are being transformed into the same image of Christ" from one degree of glory to another. **(2 Corinthians 3: 18)**

Key

==

It's always about knowing what's true, thinking rightly about that truth, i.e. rightly dividing the information and mixing faith with that truth, and finally standing our ground patiently focused on that truth—a kingdom position and posture.

Well, Pastor Ken, if this is a valid expectation to embrace.

1. Why do I struggle to experience this newness and freedom in and through my daily life?
2. Why are so many Christians still struggling with many of the same issues plaguing them now, as before?
3. Is there a real hope of living the life Jesus promised, both in this life and the life to come?" **(1 Timothy 4:8)**.

The Gideon Syndrome

JUDGES 6: 12–14.

> When the angel of the Lord appeared to
> Gideon, he said, the Lord is with you, Oh mighty
> man of valor.
>
> but Sir, "Gideon replied, "if the Lord is with
> us, why has all this happened to us? Where are all
> his wonders that our fathers told us about, when
> they said, did not the Lord bring us up out of
> Egypt? But now; the Lord has abandoned us and
> put us into the hand of Midian."
>
> the angel of the Lord turned to him and
> said, go in the strength you have, and save Israel
> out of Midian's hand, am I not sending you?"

If you continue reading in Judges 6, you would see that, like many sincere believers, Gideon's focus was on himself and his ability. Like the rest of Israel, Gideon was plagued by fear and dread.

There is a two-step pattern in which most of us engage during a time of struggle. This is a satanic process designed to keep you and I separated from God's faithfulness and imprisoned as slaves. I refer to this as "The Gideon Syndrome," and many times like you, I've found myself infected by it.

First, fear and dread has accessed Gideon's life as a result of him comparing himself and his ability against that of his enemy. He was self-focused—in this case, attempting to see himself delivering Israel from the hand of the ruthless Midianites. Going through this process, it became overwhelmingly clear that he was no match for this necessary task.

Secondly, While engaging this process, Gideon's view of God's faithfulness is diminished. And because of his focus, he now concludes that God has abandoned him. His proof is being confirmed by his present circumstances.

This is a classic definition and expression of unbelief. This same dynamic on many occasions is clearly observable in you and me?

Gideon's perception of truth is being shaped by the construct of his circumstance. Yet the Lord has said, "I've already provided everything you need to accomplish my purpose, I am sending you, and I am with you. It's my ability not yours that guarantees your victory."

Biblical Information or Revelation?

The satanic temptations, patterns, and strategies that are set against you and me today are cloaked in different packaging, but his ingredients of deception and mayhem are still the same.

Satan only comes to steal, to kill, and to destroy. But Jesus has come so that we can have life and a more abundant life, so you and I can rest comfortably in God's kingdom principles.

> He who began the good work in you, is the one who will faithfully bring it to completion. **(Philippians 1:6)**

> Continue to work out your salvation with fear and trembling, because it is God who works in you to will and to act according to His good purpose. **(Philippians 2:12b–13)**

Think about this in **Luke 14: 28–31**:

> For which of you intending to build a tower does not sit down first and count the cost (I really think that God has counted the cost for you and me) whether he has enough to finish it unless, after he has laid the foundation and not able to finish, all who sees it begin to mock him saying; this man began to build and was not able

to finish or what king going to make war against another king does not sit down first and consider whether he is able with 10,000 to meet him who comes against him with 20,000.

Now you can be absolutely sure that God is more faithful and capable than any of the characters mentioned in this parable.

So, He who has started a good work in you can and will most certainly finish the project He began. You must believe this!

For everyone born of God overcomes the world. And this is the victory that has overcome the world, even our faith. Who is he that overcomes the world. Only he who believes that Jesus is the Son of God. (**1 John 5:4–5**)

Key

===

Being new creations in Christ Jesus, the greater one lives in us. This is a spiritual reality, but for it to become your daily experience, you must continually mix faith with this truth, so that it becomes and remains fresh revelation in and through you.

God's kingdom keys are provided for His children's use—i.e. you and me. So, beloved, consider carefully each word of the Lord, which unlocks your freedom.

Insights That Can Release Your Freedom

So; He got into a boat, crossed over, and came to His own city.

then behold, they brought to Him a paralytic lying on the bed. When Jesus saw their faith, He said to the paralytic, "Son, be of good cheer; your sins are forgiven you."

And at once some of the scribes said within themselves, "this man blasphemes!"

But Jesus, knowing their thoughts, said, "why do you think evil in your hearts?

Which is easier, to say, "your sins are forgiven you, or to say, "arise and walk"?

But that you may know that the Son of Man has power on earth to forgive sins"-then He said to the paralytic, "arise, take up your bed, and go to your house."

and he arose and departed to his house.

Now when the multitude saw it, they marveled and glorified God, who had given such authority to men. **(Matthew 9:1–8)**

They brought to him a paralytic, either partial or total, it makes no difference because when coming to Jesus, the depth, the magnitude, or the age (i.e., the length of time of your struggle) has no bearing on Jesus's willingness or his ability to release you.

Man lying on a bed is a physical representation of a spiritual condition. We were all completely paralyzed; and we were all symptomatically blind, deaf, and dumb from the byproducts of sin and death.

When Jesus saw their faith ("their" is a third person pronoun and includes all involved, i.e., all the men), they were demonstrating faith in Jesus.

Though Jesus is full of perfect compassion, sympathy, and every human emotion and kindness, it was only when he saw their faith that his focus was captured with his willingness to respond to them which resulted in their needs being met by the power of the Holy Spirit.

What was it Jesus actually saw?

The Gospel of Mark has an account of this same event, and in chapter 2, says, "That the men tore a section of the roof open, and Lowered the paralytic man down in front of Jesus."

Such provocative and presumptuous behavior can easily be considered and understood as the classic demonstration of faith.

However, on more than one occasion in the Gospels, we can see episodes of people, displaying extraordinary efforts to get Jesus's attention or to demonstrate their Great love for Him.

Now, on the surface, it might appear that their efforts are why Jesus is responding to them, i.e., Jesus is equating faith with their efforts, but is that true? Remember, only truth releases us.

Let's view this thought in the setting of **Mark 5: 21–36**:

> When Jesus had again crossed over by boat to the other side of the lake, a large crowd gathered around him while he was by the lake. Then one of the synagogue rulers, named Jairus, came there. Seeing Jesus, he fell at His feet and pleaded earnestly with him, "my little daughter is dying.

Please come and put your hands on her so that she will be healed and live." So Jesus went with him. A large crowd followed and pressed around him.

A woman was there who had been subject to bleeding for 12 years.

She had suffered a great deal under the care of many doctors and had spent all she had, yet instead of getting better she grew worse. When she heard about Jesus, she came up behind him in the crowd and touched his cloak, because she thought, "if I just touch his clothes, I will be healed." immediately her bleeding stopped and she felt in her body that she was freed from her suffering.

At once Jesus realized that power had gone out from him. He turned around in the crowd and asked, "who touched my clothes?" His disciples answered, "you see the people crowding against you, and yet you can ask, who touched me?" But Jesus kept looking around to see who had done it

Then the woman, knowing what happened to her, came and fell at his feet and, trembling with fear, told him the whole truth.

He said to her, "Daughter, your faith has healed, you go in peace and be freed from your suffering." While Jesus was still speaking, some men came from the house of Jairus, the synagogue ruler. "Your daughter is dead," they said. "Why bother the teacher anymore?" Ignoring what they said, Jesus told the synagogue ruler, "Don't be afraid, just believe."

This woman's action demonstrates great effort, personal risk, and sacrifice; however, her focus was on the hem of His garment. Under Jewish law, it would've been illegal for her to knowingly place herself in a public setting where she would be physically in contact with others. She would've been considered as unclean.

Key

===

> Please note that Jesus was not conscious of the intensity of her struggle to touch Him (human effort). He was only conscious that someone touched him in faith. Everything about Jesus, His person, purpose, and power, recognizes faith.

Faith exposes our hearts to God, releasing His "kingdom to come, and His will to be done on earth" **(Matthew 9:2)**.

Was the physical efforts, the faith that Jesus saw?

I am certain this was not the case, it was not as if Jesus interpreted their extraordinary efforts and labor alone as faith.

Men judge by outward appearances and external behaviors, but God observes and judges by the internal condition of our hearts, always from the inside out and not the outside in.

Jesus is always seeing the invisible for only in that dimension is the substance of faith identifiable, this is what prompts his response to their needs as well and ours.

Not by might nor by power but by my Spirit
saith the Lord. **(Zachariah 4:6b)**

A Prophetic Overview of Jesus' Nature

A shoot will come up from the stump of Jesse; from his roots a branch will bear fruit." The Spirit of the Lord will rest on Him-the Spirit of wisdom and of understanding, the Spirit of counsel and of might, the Spirit of the knowledge and the fear of the Lord-and He will delight in the fear of the Lord. He will not judge by what He sees with His eyes, or decide by what He hears with His ears; but with righteousness He will judge the needy, with justice He will give decisions for the poor of the earth. He will strike the earth with the rod of His mouth; with the breath of His lips He will slay the wicked. **(Isaiah 11: 1–4)**

We could spend a considerable amount of time, discussing the truths spoken in this "prophetic text," but in brief, here's a couple of highlights,

It is very clear that Jesus would not make judgments or consider things through physical evidence—"what He sees with his eyes and what He hears with his ears, but with righteous judgments."

Key

===

> All His responses, even those directed towards you and
> me, are still His response to the substance of faith (a spiri-
> tual force) being mixed with His truth in our hearts.

Jesus, seeing the events unfolding in front of Him, clearly rec-
ognizes the severity of their need, so He responds to them with a
word of deliverance and healing.

(Son) relational—this young man was related to God through
Abraham. You and I, however, are blood relatives through faith in
Jesus's own blood.

Second, "take courage," don't be anxious, worried, or timid
because, your sins are forgiven"

Key

===

The severity of his physical condition does not matter; his deliverance is accomplished through the same mechanism as yours and
mine and that is this—sin is forgiven in and through Jesus.

This truth is no small matter, this is not just theology or doc-
trine, this is the key to everything. Sin is forgiven.

> Therefore, just as sin entered the world
> through one man, and death through sin, and
> in this way, death came to all men, because all
> sinned. **(Romans 5:12)**

In short, death and destruction originates with Adam's sin, so in
that instant, God's creative order is contaminated and corrupt. Every
evil and lustful impulse, known and unknown, has license to impose
and express itself in and through all of humanity.

Adam's sin gave Satan legal authority to introduce his nature and character into Adam's bloodline, infecting all mankind with death. Again, every negative physiological, psychological, or biological experience was given birth through the womb of Adam's sin.

The Body and Blood of Jesus—the Antidote

> Therefore, when He came into the world He said: "sacrifice and offering You did not desire, but a body You have prepared for Me" then He said, "behold, I have come to do Your will, O God." He takes away the first (old covenant) that He may establish the second (new covenant) and by that will, we have been sanctified through the offering of the body of Jesus Christ once for all.
> **(Hebrews 10:5, 9, 10)**

In the context of Jesus's statement, "Son, your sins are forgiven," let's consider God's authorial intent, i.e., what is God's original purpose and construct with respect to Jesus as the redeemer of all mankind?

It is understood by all that God is whole, complete, and perfect. There are no inadequacies, no mistakes, no surprises, no corrections, or adjustments to any purpose, plan, or strategy of God necessary.

He already knows the end of everything even from before it starts, and he has set His purpose and plan along with His solution in place before the first steps of any events are taken.

What Role Has God Designated Jesus to Fulfill?

Jesus has several identities, all of which are true and genuine, He fulfills and completes each identity perfectly, and each fulfilled identity is a reflection of God's heart toward you and me.

Jesus is identified as the Son of God, the savior and redeemer, the anointed one, the Messiah, the son of David, and the list goes on. There are about a hundred different designations.

But I want us to consider what I believe to be God's heart in respect to the fundamental role, purpose, and function of Jesus.

God's Sacrificial Lamb

In Old Testament types and shadows, what was the purpose and function of a lamb? What role did a lamb serve in Israel's relationship with Yahweh? And why was the sacrifice of a Lamb critical for Israel's, healing, deliverance, and protection from all their enemies?

The very first implication of a sacrifice is inferred in **Genesis 3: 21**, "where God himself seems to be providing a type of sacrifice for Adam and Eve: and the Lord God made garments of skin for Adam and his wife and clothed them."

Prior to this point in time. there was no sin, so no sacrifice (garments of skin) would've been necessary. There was no death, so no animal could die. Death only came by Adam's Sin.

Key

===

> Death has no strength or legal right to function unless it extracts its strength from sin.

This inferred sacrifice occurs after the fall of Adam. Sin and death are now online, so there is a possibility that God sacrificed an animal on the behalf of this first couple and clothed them with its skin. This, however, can only be implied in the text.

I personally believe it has legs and can stand because it fits in with every other process of sacrifice throughout the Scripture.

The second and more concrete example of a Lamb is found in **Exodus 12:1–3 NKJV**:

> And the Lord said to Moses and Aaron in Egypt, this month is to be for you the first month, the first month of your year, tell the whole community of Israel that on the 10th day of this month, each man is to take a lamb for his family, one for each household.

This appears to be the first official introduction of a lamb as the instrument of deliverance for anyone subjected to slavery and or bondages in all forms.

On the tenth day of the first month, a lamb was to be selected, i.e., Lamb selection day, everyone was to be represented by a lamb

In verse 4, it says that anyone with a hope for deliverance and freedom would have to be covered by God's purpose and designated function for the selected lamb—every individual, family, every neighbor, whosoever, Jew/ Egyptian—the Lamb was the solution.

Next, the lamb would be without blemish, the best lamb, a male of the first year, it would be sanctified or set-aside until the fourteenth day of the same month. Then at 3:00 pm, they will be simultaneously sacrificed.

> Then the whole assembly of the congregation of Israel shall kill it at twilight and they shall take some of the blood and put it on the two doorpost and on the lintel of the houses where they eat the Lamb. (**Exodus 12:7, NIV**)

We can begin to see here that God's specific purpose and function for this chosen and sanctified lamb in this context was death on the behalf of others.

> But I will pass through the land of Egypt on that night, and I will strike all the firstborn

in the land of Egypt, both man and beast; and against all the gods of Egypt, I will execute my judgment: I am the Lord.

Now the blood shall be a sign for you on the houses where you are and when I see the blood, I will pass over you, and the plague shall not be on you to destroy you, when I strike the land of Egypt. **(Exodus 12:12-13 NKJV)**

In brief, in the first eleven chapters of Exodus, ten of the most miraculous and outstanding miracles of the Bible are recorded. There were many gods in Egypt, and for our purposes, Egypt is a type of the kingdom of this world.

I believe through these ten miracles, God challenged and defeated the ten most powerful gods in Egypt—the sun god, water god, the fertility god etc. But none of these miracles from Him brokered any freedom or deliverance for His people. As a side note, God has never ordained miracles, as His source for deliverance and freedom for any people.

Because God had pre-ordain before the foundation of the world a lamb as His choice and the only source of full and complete deliverance for this world.

Now when most think of deliverance and power in the context of warfare, one would think of the Marines, the Navy SEALs, the Green Beret, etc. Men and women of tremendous courage and power are capable of extraordinary feats of extractions and rescues.

So, in contrast, a lamb would be a foolish choice to express power and victory in warfare, "But the foolishness of God is wiser than the wisdom of men."

Here are a few character traits, regarding the nature of sheep:

First of all, sheep are not like goats, cows, dogs or any other domesticated or wild animal, sheep are unique. Sheep have a strong instinct to follow the sheep in front of them—where one goes, they all go. Sheep are known to walk of cliffs, many an Australian sheepherder has had to steer the sheep away from a cliff because if one went off, several would follow. This instinct is hardwired into their nature.

Sheep are gregarious, and they are highly social and will usually stay together in a group while grazing. As a matter of fact, sheep can become highly agitated if separated from the group.

Sheep seem to sense safety by grouping together. Sheep are a natural prey, and they have no defensive mechanisms except to flee when being attacked. When sheepherders have smaller flocks, to reduce stress, they will sometimes use mirrors, so when the sheep see their reflections, they feel the flock is significantly larger, it de-stresses them. Some researchers have suggested the possibility that sheep have one of the lower IQs. They are always in need of a shepherd. Lastly, sheep will usually not flee or react violently when being slaughtered.

So, through the weakness and smallness of a lamb, God Almighty demonstrates his mighty power and great wisdom.

These are all types and shadows of the one who was to come, and all the types and shadows are fulfilled and completed in one person, Jesus Christ.

So, from before the beginning, God's primary purpose for Jesus was that of a lamb who would function as a sin barer and take upon His own body, all sin, and its punishment—thereby removing sin and the punishment from the guilty party (you and me), allowing the Guilty party to go free.

> The next day John saw Jesus coming toward him, and he said, "behold! The Lamb of God who takes away the sin of the world! **(John 1:29)**

I am convinced that Scripture makes this clear in several different locations, e.g.

> **1Peter 1:18–20** "For you know that it was not with perishable things such as silver or gold

that you were redeemed from the empty way of life handed down to you from your forefathers, but with the precious blood of Christ, the lamb without blemish or defect. He was chosen before the creation of the world but was revealed in these last times for your sake. (**1 Peter 1:18–20**)

See also **Revelations 13:8**.

So, God's primary purpose and function for Jesus was that of the sacrificial lamb, chosen by Him from before the foundation of the world.

Though He perfectly fulfilled all the types and shadows pointing toward himself, His primary assignment (being the lamb) was always functioning just below the surface.

All of Jesus's ministry flowed out from this primary function, even before the cross, the authority of the Lamb as his calling is revealed in how he relates to people.

He is always offering forgiveness of sin and the resulting deliverance from the powers of darkness, i.e., sickness, disease, and demonic activity.

Which Is Easier—
Forgiveness or Healing?

Upon Jesus declaring to the paralytic, "Your sins are forgiven," the Pharisees were offended, for they mused to themselves, "Who can forgive sins but God alone?"

But Jesus, being aware of their internal conflict, continues.

> Why do you think evil in your hearts? Which is easier; to say "your sins are forgiven you, or to say, arise and walk? But that you may know that the Son of Man has power on earth to forgive sins, he now addresses the paralytic "arise, take your bed, and go home. (**Matthew 9:4–7**)

Statements, such as this one, "Your sins are forgiven," serves as an active demonstration of Jesus, functioning as the Lamb of God, taking away sin and its fruit/side-effect, namely sickness and disease.

Now, because of the influence of the law, there is embedded in the Jewish culture this awareness that one of the consequences of sin is sickness and disease (see **John 9:1–12**).

For the purpose of our discussion, I will refer to sickness, etc., as "fruit" and define it as an external symptom or outward appearance, resulting from an internal condition (please refer to this definition regularly).

Key

==

> Jesus never judges from the fruit of anything but from the root of everything. Like the Holy Spirit, Jesus's axe is always laid to the root of the tree.

So, Jesus lays his ax to this root by declaring this man's sin to be forgiven.

Key

==

> Whenever anything is separated from a root, its fruit will wither and eventually ceased to exist, i.e., die.

Therefore, Jesus says, "What is easier to say your sins are forgiven? Or to say take up your bed and go home." His authority to forgive sin (as God's Lamb) disarms paralysis, which no longer has legal authority over this forgiven man, who can now just take his bed and go home.

And if you have opened your heart to receive Jesus Christ as your redeemer and savior, you have become a brand-new creation. And just like this forgiven man, you also being forgiven, can go home free from the works and the strategies of the kingdoms of darkness because of the authority of Jesus, the "Lamb of God," to take away all sin, even yours.

So, What Is Sin?

There is something that I personally refer to as "presumptive understanding." There is a good possibility that this is not an actual term.

So, let me define this for you. In the information-filled environment, in which we live today, you and I are easily overexposed to all forms of knowledge. This abundant supply of information, combined with an appetite for more understanding, is not a bad thing; however, in my opinion, it has created a real problem. It has and continues to have a dramatic impact on "meaning," thereby having a negative impact on our ability to respond properly to the information.

I believe this is what **Daniel 12:4** is inferring, "But you, Daniel, shut up the words, and seal the book until the time of the end; for many shall run to and from and knowledge shall increase."

It is impossible to know someone or to have relationship with them without knowing what is meant by what they say and do, especially what they say.

Remember, truth is what God said is not what I think He said, truth is what God means is not what I think He means."

Now with this being said, let's consider our question, "what is sin?"

The word, "sin," when used throughout the Scripture, is both a noun and a verb. Now this is not an attempt with this statement at being a grammatical police officer. As a matter of fact, I now beg your forgiveness for my grammatical inexperience, but nonetheless, I press on

You and I are being filled with God's Spirit of wisdom and the revelation in the knowledge of Him (Jesus), so that the eyes of our understanding are continually being opened. This process is significantly enriched by us, recognizing the word, "sin," as both a noun and a verb.

So Easily Entangled?

Hebrews 12:1 says, "Since we are surrounded by so great a cloud of witnesses, let us lay aside every weight, and the sin (noun) which so easily ensnares us."

Consider carefully this next point, the Greek word translated here as "ensnare," and in some translations "to entangle," is of a very specific nature. It is the word, EU-PE-RIS-TA-TOS, this is the only place in the New Testament this word is used.

It has the sense of skillfully encircling on all sides to attack for the purpose of inhibiting targeted actions.

In my opinion, there is such an intentional, pre-determined strategy that is set in motion here. Satan's sole purpose is to undermine and derail the expansion and authority of the kingdom of God at work in and through you and me.

Romans 7:21 says, "So I find this law at work: when I want to do good, evil is right there with me."

Who would've thought that such a simple three-letter word, "sin," could be filled with such catastrophic chaos? A word that has had an effect on every dimension of human existence.

Sin's Origin

The very first man was custom-made and hand-crafted by God.

From (Adam) to the last man to be born on the earth, whoever he might be, sin and death has legal authority over him, and there will always be the literal confrontation of good vs. evil within.

Sin has extraordinary access to you and me. It is not second nature to us but has become our only nature. Adam, who was created by God, unwittingly allowed himself to be influenced by Satan, so much so that Satan's sinful nature assumed control and management of all humanity, and creation.

So, all the seed from Adam's loins and eggs from Eve's womb became the source of humanity's infection with the first incurable disease. It is the most highly contagious of any disease that has ever existed or will ever exist. It has an instant 100 percent effective kill rate—anyone being produced from the blood of Adams loins through the womb of Eve is born dead, no hope of escape and no temporary reprieve. Some of the symptoms are fear, shame, intense torment, torture, deception, violence, known and unknown perversion, corruption, and then an eternity in hell. This is just a brief glimpse at the affects and effects of sin (the noun).

Romans 6:23 says, "For the wages of sin is death, but the free gift of God is eternal life." Because we are all born with this infectious disease working in us, humanity has been transformed from God's created form to another form. We have become the primary habitation for sin. So, everything about us is compatible with everything about sin. We can consciously or unconsciously make internal adjustments, granting sin full and complete expression through us.

The apostle Paul's internal struggle with sin is a reflection of and mirrors our experience with sin exactly.

So I find this law at work: when I want to do good, evil is right there with me.

In my inner being I delight in God's law;

But I see another law at work in the members of my body, waging war against the law of my mind and making me a prisoner of the law of sin at work within my members.

What a wretched man I am! Who will rescue me from this body of death?

Thanks be to God-through Jesus Christ our Lord! So then, I myself in my mind, am a slave to God's law, but in the sinful nature I am a slave to the law of sin. **(Romans 7:21–25 NIV)**

In the context of our response to the question, what is sin? Let's ask a second question, Is there a difference between the fruit of sin and sin itself?

I believe there is a very distinct difference between the fruit of sin and sin itself. For the sake of context in this presentation, I would like for us to consider these two in this manner.

First, sin being the root, originating from Adam and is the noun form of the word, "Hamartia." Second, sin, in its verb form, Hamartano (i.e., the action of the noun), is the fruit or the harvest from the root—our moment by moment behaviors.

We all tend to focus on the things, which are seen, i.e., physical experiences. We all tend to make most of our judgments within this structure and the physical evidence it constantly provides.

I believe this distinction is central to our understanding, practical in its application, critical to our prayer life, and essential to our foundation as we stand our ground in faith and patience.

Romans 12:2 says, "Do not be conformed to this world, but be transformed by the renewing of your mind, so that you may prove what is that good and acceptable and perfect will of God."

In preparation for this presentation I discovered that most of the respected material and commentaries that I viewed, considered sin, from its verb form only (Hamartano).

Just like most of us, we view sin and define it as things that we do that we should not do. Behaviorally base, a non-sanctioned activity.

Hamartano is the verb form of the word, "sin." It is generally defined in this manner to miss the mark, to miss the target, to miss the standard established by God, and to deviate from God's goal and not share in the prize.

Some additional clarity is added to this definition in

> And from their cities at that time the children of Benjamin number 26,000 men who drew the sword, besides the inhabitants of Gibeon, who numbered 700 select men.
>
> Among all this people were 700 selectmen who were left-handed; everyone could sling a stone and a here's breath and not miss. (**Judges 20:15–16**)

Because you and I are constantly missing the mark in our thoughts, words, and deeds, we are very conscious of unsolicited sinful behaviors (Hamartano) present and active in us.

And so, on most occasions, we apply our own personal methodology, attempting to keep ourselves from these behaviors. Whether or not we recognize this process, we are practicing self-reliance, the dependency upon personal ability, and self-management to keep ourselves holy and righteous before God.

This Behavior Has at Least Two Categories of Fruit

First is condemnation and discouragement. As we become increasingly frustrated in our efforts of self-governance, our experience becomes personal defeat and failure. This course of action restricts our ability for mixing faith with truth.

Second is pride and hypocrisy. **Romans 12:3** says, "For I say, through the grace given to me, to everyone who was among you, not to think of himself more highly than he ought to think, but to think soberly, because God has dealt to each one a measure of faith."

Being delivered from sin (noun) has its origin in the work started in Christ Jesus, being empowered by the Holy Spirit. It is not now maintained by or through my personal focus and determination.

The entire six chapters of the book of Galatians addresses this concept redundantly and with clarity.

Galatians 3:1–5 is a snapshot of the entire book:

> Oh, foolish Galatians! Who has bewitched you that you should not obey the truth, before whose very eyes Jesus Christ was clearly portrayed among you as crucified?
>
> This only I want to learn from you: did you receive the Holy Spirit by the works of the law, or by the hearing of faith?
>
> Are you so foolish? That having begun in the Holy Spirit, are you now being made perfect by the flesh? (Human effort/personal strength)

If you suffered so many things in vain-if indeed it was in vain?

Therefore he who supplies the Holy Spirit to you and works miracles among you, does he do it by the works of the law, or by the hearing of faith.

Key

==

We, as believers, must always remember because God is perfect. He can only accept perfection. **Psalms 127:1** says, "Unless the Lord builds the house Anyone who's laboring to build, labors in vain."

So, we've talked a little about Hamartano, the verb form of the word, "sin." We understand it specifically as what we do, say, or think—our actions—the sinful behaviors, which are represented through a complete physical environment and construct.

Now Let's Look at the Noun Form

Hamartia being born in a perpetual state of opposition to "God's righteousness," originating from Adam's sin.

Just think about the first part of the definition of Harmatia (the noun form) for a moment. There is a clear implication that this form of the word, "sin,: has more to do with how we were born than what we say or do—behavior. The second part, it originates and is directly related to the impact of Adam's fall. This is crucial to our understanding because it points directly as to how we are thinking about sin of any kind.

All humanity is born infected with Adam's blood, but as new creations in Christ Jesus, we are born again through the sinless blood of Jesus. His blood cleanses and purifies us from Adam's infection, freeing us from the affects and effects of his inherited sinful nature.

Key

==

If we are free from the root, we are free from the fruit.

Okay, Pastor Ken, I understand what you're saying, but what does this look like in my daily life? And how can I apply it in a practical manner, helping me live the life Jesus has for me?

Let's go back to **Matthew 9:1–8**. There is a key here, which must be recognized, but as with any key, it has no value or effect if not inserted into something, which is locked then turned to unlock it. The whole purpose of any key is for the locking or unlocking of something.

You can have the keys to your prison door and still not use them, thereby remaining a prisoner.

As I've stated earlier regarding a concern of mine, there is in today's environment a wealth of accurate biblical information; however, what is required in addition to this information is Revelation, which will ultimately lead to a demonstration of God's kingdom at work in you and me.

I have come to understand this basic fact that after some forty years of being in the family of God, you and I can easily stumble over the things of God, not because of their complexity, but because of their simplicity. Even when God choses to hide things, they are still "revealed to you and me"—His children.

God is not in the business of making things complex, complicated, or confusing, so that only a handful of selected specially trained people can understand what He is saying.

Remember, "whosoever will may come" and "he who has an ear to hear, let him hear what the Spirit of the Lord is saying to the church"—that's you and me.

In the new covenant, God by the Holy Spirit speaks to all His children, not just to those who are perceived as highly regarded.

Just be open to listen and hear by the way, sometimes, hearing can be just an acknowledgement of sound, but listening implies a deliberate focus on what's being said with the intention of understanding. This primarily occurs in an environment of humility.

So, let's take a quick review to identify the keys and then consider some practical ways to apply them, activating in you and me, the genuine experience of being unlocked as we faithfully pursue our father's business.

===

Jesus, having completed His first major discourse(the sermon on the mount/**Matthew 5–7**), is now en route to his hometown of Capernaum. Multitudes are now being exposed to His authoritative teaching, governing the dynamics of the kingdom of God.

He enters a fishing boat and crosses over the Sea of Galilee to the shores of his hometown, Capernaum. After a few days, Jesus is teaching in a house, and a multitude, consisting of the Pharisees, the Sadducees, along with many or most from his hometown and sur-rounding villages, have created a massive crowd.

Luke 5:17 says, "And the power of the Lord was present to heal them."

During this event, some men come bringing with them a friend, who is being tortured by paralysis. Initially, they sought to bring him in through the crowd on the ground floor, but because of the conges-tion and the multitude of people, they were unable to do so. Being determined, they went up on the roof, made an opening, and low-ered the man from the roof into Jesus's presence and no doubt in the view of everyone present.

Now, we get a glimpse of the first part of the key and when Jesus saw their faith. I believe we've already made a brief and relatively clear case for an argument that faith is the singularly fundamental ingredient for any understanding or application of God's truth.

And secondly, that their efforts and determination was not the primary evidence of the faith Jesus saw.

There were, I'm sure, many people present who saw the physical efforts displayed be these men as impressive. Being convinced that the reason Jesus responded to them had everything to do with their extraordinary efforts. Wow! They worked so hard.

Just like many who will read this text and presume that Jesus saw their efforts as their faith, so likewise many of those being pres-ent would've viewed their efforts in a similar light.

Remember, men observe outward appearances and have a high regard for such, but God is always evaluating internal dynamics mainly heart condition.

Key

===

> Remember **Hebrews 4:2**, "The gospel was preached to us as well as to them; but the word, which they heard, (biblical information) did not profit them because they did not mix faith with what they heard."

Faith in the context of this this understanding cannot be over-stated, it bears constant repetition. Because of our fallen natures, we tend to forget God's benefits, which are always available and freely given to all. Consider **Psalms 103:2–3**, "Bless the Lord, O my soul, and forget not all his benefits: who forgives all your iniquities, who heals all your diseases (present tense)."

Jesus continues saying, "Your sins are forgiven" now Jesus being "God's chosen Lamb before the foundation of the world." Even here before the cross, He demonstrates the Father's purpose in Him by removing the punishment of sin—sickness from this man.

Please note it is the noun form of the word Sin (hamartia), that is being used here, Remember the definition.

Hamartia is being born in a perpetual state of opposition to "God's Righteousness," originating from Adam's sin.

Think about the setting in which Jesus makes such a statement. He's speaking to total strangers, being scrutinized by many of the theological masters (scribes and Pharisees) who thoroughly under-stand the law and the commandments. To paraphrase what I believe Jesus is saying, He's speaking as God's chosen Lamb/authorized by God to remove sin. He's speaking to someone under sins legal authority, being tortured and paralyzed.

All sickness and disease, everything negative, has legal expression because of sin. What do you think the focus was of the men who came to Jesus? I believe they came in the hope of being healed and delivered from the torture and paralysis of his daily life.

Jesus, seeing their faith, answers their prayer by addressing the root of the problem and not the fruit of the problem. Jesus says, "Son," inferring relationship. I am releasing you from the state in which you were born that of being in opposition to God's righteousness, which originates from Adam's sin.

This man's entire life was being severed from sin, originating from Adam, which means the paralysis torturing him, or any kind of sickness, no longer has legal authority to impose itself in this man's life.

This man's paralysis drew its right of enforcement from sin, originating with Adam's initial failure. Sickness and disease are the side effects of that event.

The effects of the fall of Adam continued to have full, uninterrupted right of enforcement until the death and resurrection of Jesus. So, this man's sickness had the legal right to bring death and destruction on him and all of humanity.

But once sin is removed as the reigning power by God's Lamb, who willingly takes upon Himself the Sin, (noun) of the world, sickness or any of the fruit of sin can no longer derive its power from Adam's original Sin. Sin is cut off from its root. No wonder the Pharisees and the Sadducees were highly offended and murmured in their heart—"who can forgive sin but God alone." Jesus's focus on the sin of this man's life had nothing to do with the verb form of the word, "sin" (Hamartano)—any of his bad behavior, thoughts, or actions.

Most of our thinking regarding sin (behaviorally based) is consumed by our efforts of warring against, railing against, and desperately attempting to manage or eliminate sin—bad behavior—from our lives and the lives of others.

Sin, the verb (Hamartano), is just like the man's sickness, only symptomatic—fruit springing from a root, and Jesus always deals with the root of any issue especially sin. "Behold the Lamb of God which takes away the sin (noun) of the world."

This illustrates God's redemptive process for everyone. Anyone starting by faith and continuing to live within His construct, where forgiveness is the constant singular priority, can and will experience Gods full and complete freedom.

Matthew 9:5 says, "For which is easier to say, your sins (Noun) are forgiven? or to say, arise take up your mat and go home?"

If we are free from the root, we are free from the fruit.

A Focus On Forgiveness

Let's begin this section by being reminded of two key blocks from the foundation:

> First is **Hebrews 4:2**, "The gospel was preached to us as well as to them; but the word which they heard, (biblical information) did not profit them because they did not mix faith with what they heard."
>
> Second is "truth is what God said, not what I think He said, truth is what God means, not what I think He means."

> Jesus Christ is the same yesterday, today, and forever do not be carried about with various and strange doctrines. For it is good that the heart be established by grace, not with foods which have not profited those who have been occupied with them. **(Hebrews 13:8–9)**

There are several things that are inferred in these two verses and can be clearly corroborated and validated in other portions of Scripture. However, within the context of our discussion, I would like to highlight just a couple first in verse 8. We can see that Jesus as a person is the same and he never changes.

That being said, it is understood that God's purpose for Jesus as the lamb is offered once for all time and is continually available to whosoever. It has never changed as well. As we've already stated, Jesus is the same, and His function is the same even in our present-day moments of failure.

As we have trusted God's redemptive process from the beginning, we are to continually exercise faith in Jesus's blood, even today after the initial born-again experience.

"The just, shall live by his faith," we began by trusting, and we continue kingdom living by continued trusting. The body that Jesus offered, and the blood he poured out, is just as fresh and powerful today (in this moment and all future ones), as it was when the first drop was spilled some two thousand years ago on Golgotha's Hill.

Jesus's blood is still pooling, fresh on God's altar, in God's presence. It is not affected by bacteria, and it is not contaminated with any corruption, decay, or foul odor, for these would be the by-products of Adam's sin.

In Matthew chapter 8, the leper came to Jesus, full of leprosy, which is a picture of sin (noun)—originating from Adam (the sick is to be "healed, but lepers, are to be cleansed").

The disease of leprosy is highly contagious, so much so that lepers were required to cry out, "Unclean! Unclean!" and maintain the distance of a fifty-foot radius under normal conditions, an, as much as two hundred feet on a windy day. Yet again, in this episode, God's love and redemption is demonstrated by Jesus's actions.

Even before Jesus heals the leper, He places his hand upon him, a picture of God's compassionate heart toward those who are untouchable, odorous, corrupt, infected, and isolated.

Key

==

When anything, which is corrupt or sinful, contacts the same body Jesus offered for you and me, it doesn't infect him, it dies. Sin and death perishes once placed upon the body of Jesus, and His sinless righteous blood cleanses us, declaring us to be righteous.

Remember this, Jesus's blood doesn't just declare us as not guilty as in being acquitted. It says, "That we were never guilty, there was never a charge against us."

We have become the righteousness of God in Christ Jesus, just like Jesus is not guilty having never sinned **Matthew 27: 4b** says, "I have betrayed innocent blood."

Anyone who understands and trust God's purpose for the body and blood of Jesus is judged in the same light as Jesus—not guilty—having never sinned.

> Love has been perfected among us in this: that we may have boldness in the day of judgment; because as he is, so are we in this world. **(1 John 4:17 NKJV)**

This position can only be entered into through the exercise of faith, and so likewise one must continue in that same faith being anchored and established in God's righteousness.

Key

==

Any deviation from trusting God's process, no matter how sincere we might be, derails us from His righteousness and places us under the management of "the works of the flesh" i.e.—our own perception of what is good.

Many sincere and genuine believers labor under the assumption that rolling up their sleeves, getting down to God's business and giving oneself completely in the fight against sin (the verb form Hamartano) is how we are to honor and pleased God.

They believe that through self-effort and rigorous disciplines, God is pleased. Even though these efforts are riddled with repetitive failure, guilt, shame, and hypocrisy, they are continued and are highly regarded by many. Some would say, "Well, no one is perfect," "God knows my heart," and "faith without works is dead." Now at face value, these actions look and sound reasonable. One could almost imagine God observing these earnest efforts with a smile on His face, indicating His acceptance of the offerings of broken and corrupt self-effort.

Our loving, righteous, and Holy God is perfect, and so is everything related to Him and His kingdom. All of His provisions are perfect, and everything offered to Him must also be perfect. God is not offering wholeness and perfection just to receive corruption, ineptness, and inadequacy in return. He requires wholeness, but unfortunately our wholeness is never enough.

Consider this thought—on the third day of creation, God introduces this principle, "Every seed would reproduce according to its kind." This principle is implied again in Galatians 6 where Paul says, "Whatever a man sows that is what he shall also reap." There is no double standard in the kingdom of God, and God himself is not double minded. He would not sow wholeness, completeness, and fullness in you and me and be pleased receiving back from us imperfection, unsoundness, and incompleteness.

I think we imagine God as saying, "They only scored an eighty-five on that test, they were so sincere, so I'll accept it as one hundred. God does not grade anything on the curb."

Key

===

If the only requirement for pleasing God was trying really hard to do your best, there would've been no reason for Jesus to come.

Our best and most sincere efforts would've been good enough and acceptable to Him, but beloved, that is not the case. So, in the context of our discussion, consider these two scriptures:

> This is the word of the Lord to Zerubbabel: not by might nor by power, but by my Spirit says the Lord of host. **(Zachariah 4:6)**

> Unless the Lord builds the house, they labor in vain who build it; unless the Lord guards the city, the watchman stays awake in vain. **(Psalms 127:1)**

God can only accept the work of his own hand and that is the work that he has begun in you through Christ Jesus—the perfect work of Christ.

Philippians 1:6 says, "He who has begun the work, is the one who continues the work bringing it to completion."

In the light of this consider **John 1:10–13**:

> He was in the world, and the world was made through him, and the world did not know him. He came to his own, and his own did not receive him.
>
> But as many as received him, to them he gave the right to become children of God, to those who believe in his name: who were born, not of blood, nor of the will of the flesh, nor of the will of man, but of God.

I believe there is a principle hidden within this text that can readily be applied and thereby impacting our relationship with the Holy Spirit and, the work He's begun and continues to do in you and me. I do not believe it to be an exaggeration, or the manufacturing of a supportive position.

Notice the first parallel in verses 10–11. He's in the world, He's made everything and yet the world does not know Him. He then comes to his own and just like the world, His own does not, cannot receive Him. The application here is this: even though God has begun the work in you and me, we can position ourselves in such a way, that His work is impeded, effectively having its development stunted.

Verse 12 implies as many as received him—anyone who lives in an agreeable manner through faith in His working in us is being changed, and something is becoming in them, and in verse 13, "and that which is becoming in them," is not a product of human effort i.e. "the will of man" self-efforts but of God.

With that said Hebrews chapters 3 to 4 reminds us again that a Sabbath rest has been designated for New Covenant believers.

So, what is a Sabbath rest? How does it relate to our present-day experience? And what is the impact both immediate and long-term, on you and me, within the context of our discussion?

Lastly, how do we enter and live this life out of this "Sabbath Rest?"

What Is a Sabbath Rest?

> Wisdom is the principal thing; therefore, get wisdom. And in all your getting, get understanding. **(Proverbs 4:7)**

> Let us therefore labor, (work really hard) to enter into God's rest. **(Hebrews 4:11)**

This statement is an oxymoron and can easily become confusing, but only if we define God's rest as literally doing nothing. Please note as with any direction from the Lord, there must always be the application of faith being mixed with his instruction.

So, all works of righteousness are to be the work of entering into God's rest—a continual reliance upon what He has done, not on what you and I accomplish by hard work and focus.

Hebrews 4:10 says, "For he who has entered His/God's rest, has himself also ceased from his own works as God did from his."

Now again, the idea of ceasing from our own efforts of "trying to be enough" tends to foster internal contradictions, generating pressure for us to take some kind of action.

In conjunction with trying to earn God's acceptance, there is also a subtle behind the scene working of Satan. He's always working just below the surface of our conscious minds, continuously pressing you and me into various types of religious behavior.

Some of these are bold and obvious, and some are abstract and almost imperceptible, but God sees everything clearly and only responds to genuine faith.

Remember **Matthew 9:2**, "When Jesus saw their faith?" It was not their efforts, in other words, "the hard work of getting their friend to Jesus" that prompted a response from Him, it was their faith. So, likewise, it will be your faith, not your good works or best efforts, that elicits His divine interaction on your behalf.

Continuing in the instruction from **Proverbs 4:7** let's focus our thinking and understanding on the development of God's people, in the matter of entering into his sabbath rest.

Let's start by considering these two words; first the word, "Sabbath," the first occasion for the use of this word in scripture is in **Genesis 2:2 (NKJV)**, "And on the seventh day God ended his work which he had done, and he rested on the seventh day, from all his work which he had done."

Now interestingly enough, the word, "Sabbath," meaning to rest (from work), to cease, to stop, to be absent, to come to an end, to perish, and finally, to celebrate, is a Hebrew verb

It is a word that describes an intentional action, a state of being, or the production of a result. It is translated over seventy times in the Old Testament as to cease, with the idea of coming to the end of labor in all of its many forms, with an inference of rejoicing that the task is completed.

Please note that during the six days of creation, on almost every occasion, at the end of the day's work, the Holy Spirit used this phrase to describe it, "and God saw that it was Good." You can almost imagine God musing over the day's work and saying, "Ah its perfect."

Consider this example—a woman for nine months, carrying a baby, and just prior to delivery, she goes into labor. Once the birthing process is completed, and the delivery has come, she enters a state of rest, usually with a sense of celebration, Sabbath.

The scriptures declare very clearly that the process of ceasing from work for a final time was introduced on day number seven of creation.

Unfortunately, some theological positions tend to make the seventh day itself overly sacred. Whenever we religiously assume this theological posture, we are motivated by our fixation on day number 7 instead of comprehending God's actions—i.e. the event that made the day holy and dynamic.

As a matter of fact, one could technically argue that days 1–6 each contained a brief glimpse of the seventh day. What I mean is this, the work of each day comes to an end, and then God for that day ceases to work **(Gen. 1:5, 8, 13, 19, 23, 31.)** So, the evening and the morning were." He is establishing a period set aside for work and one set aside for Rest.

Jesus states in **John 11: 9–10**, "Are there not 12 hours of daylight set aside for work" but night comes when no one can or does any work"

The inference is days are for working and evenings for resting. Now this and similar language is used at the end of each day, and God ceases work at the end of each day. The difference being that days 1–6, God's work ceased though not fully completed, whereas the seventh day, all of creation was finalized and completed. God now enters His "Sabbath rest."

How does (entering His rest) affect our every-day experience?

> Today if you will hear his voice do not harden your hearts as in the rebellion, in the day of trial in the wilderness where your fathers tested me, tried me, and saw my works for 40 years 10 therefore I was angry with that generation and said they always go astray in their hearts, they have not known my ways. so I swore in my wrath, they shall never enter my rest. **(Hebrews 3:7)**

Remember, it is not just any rest we are called to enter in, but God's "Sabbath Rest," which is the ceasing from all works and not just some.

Hebrews is an amazing book in the Bible. It contains many Christian doctrines and divine instructions on how to live within God's supernatural kingdom. Though written to what I believe is a born-again Jewish community, it is, nonetheless, directed to new covenant believers—"New Creations in Christ Jesus"

So, the first word in **Hebrews 3:7** is "today." Question, when is today? Answer, today is always today—we are to hear what the Holy Spirit is saying today.

He instructs us, "do not harden your hearts as your brothers did during the rebellion"—as Israel did when God spoke to them in the day of their testing in the wilderness.

If we are to understand how entering His rest affects our lives today, we'll need to see this within the context of Numbers 13–15, which depicts "the Rebellion."

I would recommend a brief reading of these three exciting, animated, and informative chapters.

Please remember that God was not pleased with them because of their disobedience, I.E.—an evil heart of unbelief. So, likewise, you and I must be careful or we can become hardened by "that same evil heart of unbelief" (remember the "Gideon Syndrome"). And Just as Israel was overthrown in the wilderness, we can have a similar experience.

Now, because they refused to believe God, the obstacles they faced in the wilderness proved to be greater than their ability to stand in righteousness.

It is never God's intention that His people (you and me as well) be defeated by any challenge. This was and continues to be deeply disappointing to Him, for without faith, it is impossible to please God.

You and I must be careful because these things occurred as examples for us today. "For we are the ones on whom the end of the ages has come." We can easily trek in Israel's footsteps even though we are empowered by the Holy Spirit for victory over every obstacle we encounter in our wilderness.

They can overcome and enslave us if, we give place to the hardness of heart which comes from unbelief. So, let's not move too far away from the foundation and focus of this entire matter, which is freedom from sin—the root and the fruit.

We've already established that the word, "sin," is both a noun and a verb, and it is always the noun (hamartia) vs. the verb (Hamartano). You may think my concern and emphasis regarding this matter that sin the noun vs sin the verb is much like the Shakespearean title, "Much ado about nothing."

But on the contrary, over forty times in the book of Romans, the word, "sin," is used. Only once or twice is the verb form of the word used in the entire book. On every other occasion, when Paul is teaching us about sin, he's speaking specially about the noun form of the word (Hamartia). Hamartia, being born in a perpetual state of opposition to "God's righteousness," originated from Adam's sin.

Is this what Jesus delivered us from? If so, you and I are free from sin's root and its fruit.

We are considering the episode in **Matthew 9:1–8**. What did Jesus see when he saw the faith of the men who put forth extraordinary effort to get to him by tearing open the roof and lowering their sick companion?

Secondly, consider Jesus's response to these men, Son, your sins are forgiven," whose focus and motivation wasn't only in getting their friend to Him for honor and worship, their primary motive was to obtain healing and deliverance.

The word, "sin," here is not the verb but the noun (Harmatia). Jesus's response initially doesn't appear to have anything to do with why they came to him. Their initial desire was not "Lord, forgive us for we have sinned."

The question is this, how are we living our lives? Are we trying to live by guarding our lives from sin the verb, Harmatano? Or are we resting in Jesus's finished work by continually trusting Him for our deliverance from sin the noun, Hamartia?

This a legitimate biblical position to consider: if we are free from the root (sin the noun), then we are also free from the fruit (sin the verb). Every day of our lives is withering and will eventually cease to have expression and die.

The Scripture says, "by 2 or more witnesses every word is established," so let's see if this position can be found elsewhere in scripture being clearly established as a biblical principle. Then we can mix faith with it and practice it, thereby we experience God's freedom.

John 15: 1–8 will be discussed. "I am the true vine, and my Father is the gardener" (v. 1).

Isaiah 53:2 says, "For He shall grow up before Him as a tender plant and as a Root out of dry ground." Let's establish some identities, so going forward, we'll always know who the text is referring to.

Jesus is the vine—the true root. The Father is the vine dresser, gardener, or owner. And in this context, we are the branches. And finally, the fruit is always displayed by the branches—branches are created to showcase the fruit from the root.

> "Every branch in me that does not bear fruit
> he takes away, and every branch that bears fruit
> he prunes, that it may bear more fruit" (v. 2)

It is implied here that all branches come as a result of and are developed from the root. It is the root that produces the branch, and there is no effort required from the branch to produce itself.

Reproduction is a natural process, so likewise, when fruit comes on the branch, there is no effort by the branch to produce fruit, this is also the natural process.

There is a responsibility for every branch to bear fruit. The reason the branch exists is so that the root has a place to display its fruit. One could also infer that the branches can bear expected fruit or not. If a branch bears no fruit or another kind of fruit, the Father (the gardener), takes away or severs that branch from the vine/root. Fruitfulness is the critical component in being a part of the Root.

"And every branch that bears fruit He prunes, that may bear more fruit" (v. 2B). "My ways are not your ways saith the Lord" **(Isaiah 55)**.

God's criteria is perfection. His standard is wholeness and completeness. So, in the context of our discussion, we are expected to wholly and completely meet and fulfill His purpose and plan for us.

So, even if we are experiencing a measure of fruitfulness, His standard is still unattainable through our own giftedness, education, experiences, sincere desire, or our focused determination. Sometimes, we unwittingly begin to think within ourselves how wonderfully effective we are, and we might even include the phrase, "by the grace of God." But notice what the verse says, "That even if we are fruitful, God is continually purging us," He purifying us by removing the unnecessary twigs leaves from our lives, so that we can begin to express an even higher image of the root.

God in this process is causing you and me to be continually transformed into the very image and likeness of His Son, "from glory to glory;" therefore, self-effort is unacceptable to him. You and I do not have God's perception of wholeness, we only have our own.

Branches are continually at the mercy and grace of the one who began the work in them. They naturally trust wholeheartedly His love and faithfulness to continue and complete His purpose and perfect work in and through them.

The end results is this, you and I begin to experience an unimaginable, supernatural, and fruitful life. We are continually being transformed into the image and likeness of the root.

> "You are already clean because of the word
> which I have spoken to you" (v. 3).

If you have opened your heart to receive Jesus Christ, this divine process has already begun.

> "Abide in me, and I in you. As the branch can-
> not bear fruit of itself, unless it abides in the vine,
> neither can you, unless you abide in me" (v. 4).

The word, "abide," (meinate) is a verb, the implication is that of one actively remaining or enduring, while constantly resisting the Lure to abandon a present state of being or position.

> The branch did not establish itself in the root "you do not support the root, but the root supports you" **(Rom. 11: 18)**

The root establishes itself, and out of the root develops the branch. But once established, the branch has the option and obligation to remain in the root/vine because fruit is the product of the root and not the branch. Branches cannot produce "root fruit" on its own.

Remember, any fruit that is not "root fruit" is considered corrupt and rejected by the vinedresser—God.

Now, in the context of our present-day culture, there are many sincere believers who have a genuine heart for God, but because of a lack of clarity in this area, they are producing corrupt fruit.

That is fruit not flowing directly from the root through their lives. They are producing fruits of self-righteousness—as they imagine God to be. Consider **Romans 10:1–4**:

> Brethren, my heart's desire and prayer to God for Israel is that they may be saved for I bear them witness that they have a zeal for God, but not according to knowledge for they being, ignorant of God's righteousness, and seeking to establish their own righteousness, have not submitted to the righteousness of God.

For Christ is the end of the law for righteousness to everyone who believes.

I am the vine; you are the branches. He who abides in me, and I in him, bears much fruit; for without me you can do nothing

Unless the Lord builds the house, they who labor; labor in vain. **(Psalms 127:1)**

One of the most subtle but more significant side effects of Adam's sin was the insertion into Adam's personality, this satanic phrase, "and you shall be as God" **(Genesis. 3)**.

This is the image the serpent was impressing in Eve's mind, "Listen! If you eat of this fruit you will no longer need God to make decisions for you will be like him, knowing what's good or not. then you can make the decisions like God for yourself."

It was at this point the Scripture says, "And when the woman saw that the tree was good for food, pleasing to the eyes and make her wise."

She consumed the fruit so as t; attain that "God-like" status of self-governance, thereby enabling her to make her own choices.

Immediately afterward, she made her first "God like decision," it was to share it as a benefit with her husband, Adam, who no doubt, having been influenced by the same proposition Satan presented to Eve, ate as well.

This dynamic is at the core of all human struggle. It impedes the simplicity of trusting the faithfulness of God's redemptive process. Even as believers, we constantly attempt to impose our own ways in everything, thinking it an upgrade to God's pre-ordained structure.

Key

==

Remember, God's process is this—the root has done the work, and the branches are simply to receive the "root's work" already done.

Philippian 1:6 says, "Being confident of this very thing, that He who has begun a good work in you, will complete it, until the day of Jesus Christ."

Phrases, such as these two, "what you can" or "I can do," throughout the Scripture in my opinion, produce points of stumbling for some. I say this because of one word at the center of it all, the word, "do."

Almost always the word, "do," is defined as an action or an undertaking in which you must take charge, generally speaking, the responsibility and accomplishment of the task is focused on you. It is dependent upon your ability, your determination, your enthusiasm, and your talent.

But in the context of verse 5, "Without me you can do nothing." Let's really think about what's being said. We've already established that the "me" in the text is referring to Jesus who is the root.

We've already determined that the "you" in the text (you and me) are the branches. Branches can do nothing on their own to produce fruit. The fruit is already established in the root, so the word, "do," in this context has nothing to do with the kind of actions we (the branches) take.

Consequently, He is saying, without Me—without what's already been done in the root—you can do nothing. Branches cannot produce anything unless it's already been established in the root. Now most believers will readily acknowledge this to be so, but only seconds after that acknowledgment "without me you can do nothing," something is unconsciously, activated internally, and many of us gravitate to self-effort, attempting to accomplish the work that is Holy Spirit work.

No human effort, energy, talent, or ability of any kind or in any form, sincerity notwithstanding, is required in the accomplishment of any work of the Holy Spirit.

John 3:6 says, "That which is born of the flesh is flesh that which is born on the Spirit is spirit."

Key

===

> So, for you and me to accomplish any work by the Holy Spirit, our focus must be on what God has already completed not on myself or what I must do to accomplish it.

This is faith 101, "Without faith it is impossible to please God."

John15: 6 says, "If anyone does not abide in me, he is cast out as a branch and is withered; and they gather them and throw them into the fire, and they are burned."

Not only is fruit flowing from the root into the branches, so that "root fruit" is developed and displayed by the branch. But here, we see that the very life of the branch itself is contained and sustained in the same process.

Life-sustaining sap flows from the root through the bark of the tree and infuses life into the branches. If this natural process is altered in any way or for any reason, the branch can receive no life, and thereby have no means of producing or displaying "root fruit." In such a case, the gardener, God, will remove any branch that is not being sustained by the life flowing from the Root.

Key

==

If anything, good or bad is separated from its roots, it withers and dies, and eventually falls or is removed from existence. Fallen, disconnected dead branches, fully withered and having no "root life" present, are gathered and burned in a fire.

Revelation 2:29 says, "He who has an ear to hear let him hear what the Spirit of the Lord is saying."

> "If you abide in me, and my words abide in you, you will ask what you desire, and it shall be done for you. By this my father is glorified, that you bear much fruit; so, you will be my disciples" (vv. 7–8).

We've briefly discussed, hopefully with some clarity, our position as branches. In addition to this, we must understand our purpose and function of displaying "root fruit."

There was also a brief discussion regarding the subtlety of you and I trying to do, sincerity notwithstanding, "Holy Spirit work" hopefully seeing the futility of it. Gods view of it as corrupt, a lack of faith, and a disregard for His holy process.

These last two verses (7–8) start with a conditional term, the word, "if." "If you abide in me and my words abide in you," we can get a sense of the value God places on the function and work of faith.

"You will ask what you desire, and it shall be done for you." So, the requirement here, is not in my doing the work, it is in me "asking and trusting" His faithfulness to do the work Himself. Technically it's a work, which has already been done.

Verse 8 highlights this thought, "This is how God the father is glorified"

In the process of asking, while mixing faith with this process, we can produce and display root fruit, thereby fulfilling our roles as disciples.

As we continue our discussion to determine whether this presentation is worthy of acceptance and application, our hope is that everyone might experience the fullness of God's purpose for themselves. "For God is glorified as we bear much fruit."

John 15:16 says, "You did not choose me, but I chose you and appointed you that you should go and bear much fruit, and that your fruit should remain, that whatever you ask the father in my name he may give you."

At this moment, I would like for us in humility to evaluate the fruit we're presently displaying, keeping in mind the effectiveness of Satan's initial strategy, by which he so easily derailed Adam and Eve.

Remember, this same strategy was passed into the blood and nature of all humanity, which includes you and me. With that said, even though you and I are born again and delivered out of the kingdom of darkness, having been transferred into and under the authority of the kingdom of Jesus Christ, this satanic strategy, if we are careless, can be just as effective now as in the beginning.

This strategy is clandestine and most effective by working just beneath the surface of our motives, and it carefully cloaks itself with untruth. Are we unwittingly being corrupted and managed by this strategy? If so, why are we so vulnerable to this specific approach?

The answer continues to be found within this satanic offering, "And you shall be as God, knowing good and evil." We all tend to process this statement in this fashion

You won't need to wait on God's instructions because you yourself will know the best action to take and resolve the problem, so just evaluate these things yourself and make the same decision as God would.

So, in the light of these comments, what kind of fruit are we displaying?

Remember, God who is perfect created the man and the woman. He set them in a perfect environment. They had daily fellowship with Him in the spirit. They had authority and knowledge for subduing and managing all of God's creation, including the serpent, and yet, they were manipulated into producing corrupt fruit, which seemed right to them.

Proverbs 14:12 says, "There is a way that seems right to a man, but it ends in the way of death."

Now, let's not be so harsh on them because we tend to think, *I wouldn't have done that.* or, *Adam should've said something or done something, and we wouldn't be in this mess.*

Personally, I don't believe that to be the case with Adam, in terms of the available choices he had, but that's a discussion for another time.

My point is this, you and I are created to produce "root fruit." With that said, we are not robots and have the option for producing fruit of our own choosing—fruit that seems right to us, fruit that seems to resolve that which we perceive as problematic, and fruit appearing to be beneficial to all. But only the root can produce pure incorruptible fruit. You and I are created and called to be vessels, which (reflect and display, not manufacture) the fruit of the root. One reason for Satan's success is that his appeal is tailor-made to each individual soul.

Your mind, feelings, and emotions that special environment in which you prefer to make choices are all tailor-made just for you. This process is almost imperceptible, as I have said, this tactic is tailor-made. His strategy for you won't appeal or have any impact in me, and likewise, his strategic appeal impacting my life are tailor-made just for me, having little to no impact on you.

So, unless we remain in the root, and the root remains active and online in us, we can become vulnerable to all the wiles and strategic manipulations of the enemy.

Always remember, we are dealing with the father of trespassing a thief whose only drive and motivation is in killing and destroying. He's not playing by legal rules, and his only intention toward you and me is in taking advantage in any area of ignorance or carelessness we exhibit.

Hence the encouragement from Paul in Ephesians 6, "Be strong in the Lord and in the power of his might, and put on (keep on) the full armor of God, so that you might be able to stand your ground, and quench all the fiery darts of the evil one"—neutralizing his strategy.

So, if we are free from the root, sin the noun (Hamartia being born in a perpetual state of opposition to "God's Righteousness" originating from Adam's sin), then we are also free from the fruit sin the verb (Hamartano). So, every sinful behavior should be withering and eventually ceasing to have its routine expression in and through us.

==

1 John 3: 7–9 says, "Little children, let no one deceive you. He who practices righteousness (the willingness to live in fellowship and orderly function with the root) is righteous, just as He (Jesus) is righteous. Now he who sins (noun) is of the devil, for the devil has sinned from the beginning."

For this purpose (the neutralizing of Adams sin), the son of God was manifested, that he might destroy (to render as powerless, weak and inconsequential) the works of the devil.

Whoever or whatever (your human spirit) has been born of God does not sin for His. Jesus's seed remains in him (you and me) and he (the new creation) cannot sin (noun) because he (the new creation) has been born of God.

Adam's seed (sin the noun) has been destroyed. Through the body and blood of God's lamb, Jesus.

==

There is, however, a significant difference between knowledge and experience. There are many, many, people who have and abundant knowledge of the things of God.

But God has not established His process so that only the intellectually gifted could attain it. His process functions within the construct of faith, humility, and dependency. Whoever wants to may come, and the Holy Spirit readily reveals God's heart to him.

It is God's every intention for you and I to come to a full knowledge of truth and of equal importance is His desire is for the just to live by mixing faith with His truth.

Consider carefully these verses of Scripture in the light of our discussion.

Hebrews 11: 1–3 says, "Now faith is the substance of things hoped for Faith is the evidence of things not seen. For by it (faith) the elders obtained a good testimony."

In verse 3, by faith we understand that the world/universe was framed by the word of God (everything is set in order by His word) so that the things, which are seen (the physical natural environment) were not made of things, which are visible.

In verse 6, it says without faith, it is impossible to please Him, for everything about God, His person His wisdom, power, and love for us is so fantastical, so amazing that it is impossible for our natural intellectual minds to process the enormity or reality of God.

So, for humanity to have fellowship of any kind with God, He included in our design faith as a fundamental function in life. Hopefully, you can recognize that without the implementation of faith, we have no means of engaging let alone pleasing Him.

"For he who comes to God must believe that he is, and that he is a rewarder of those who diligently seek him."

Sometimes, the language used in an English translation conjures up ideas and notions that are not intended in the original text, such as the phrase, "diligently seek him." This phrase can easily suggest that we are to roll up our sleeves and with a determined focus, go after God.

This, however, in my opinion, is not the heart of the Lord in this matter. I am certain that in every matter requiring faith, human effort, and energy is not God's objective, as a matter of fact, human effort and energy, inhibits, erodes, and disrupts the simplicity of faith's release.

The Scripture is clear regarding this matter. Proverbs 3:5–8 says, "Trust the Lord with all of your heart And do not lean on your own understanding, in all your ways, acknowledge him and he will make your paths straight."

Verse 7 do not be wise in your own eyes through the Lord and depart from evil.

Verse 8 says it will mean health to your flesh and strength for your bones.

==

This being said, we can see now how critical the function of faith is in everything we do. Periodically, in a Bible class, I will ask this question, "What is the primary purpose for God's word with regards to our relationship to it?"

On almost every occasion, the first response that I will hear is doing it and obey it. Initially, there is truth in this response; however, in my opinion, this is not the primary purpose of God's word with regards to our relationship to.

I believe the primary purpose is this—to believe it. I believe our first response to God's word is to believe. Any attempt to do it or obey it, without first believing or trusting it, is simply works of the flesh. Its legalism run amok. This behavior is solely powered by the flesh, my sincerity, my own understanding, and finally my ability to achieve God's perfect word.

This mind-set is doomed to repetitive failure. There is a disconnect with the Holy Spirit. Remember, "the just shall live by faith— from faith to faith"

So, let's think again about what I believe is the fundamental key to the whole matter if we are free from the root, sin the noun (Hamartia). Then we are also free from the fruit sin the verb (Hamartano), so every sinful behavior should be withering and eventually ceasing to have its routine expression through us.

Let's do a brief and final review of our position after this—our focus will be on application—how do we began to live out in a practical way the things that we've asserted.

The First Position Is Major (Everything Starts with Truth)

Numbers 23:19 says, "God is not like man that he should lie nor the Son of Man that he should change his mind, he has never spoken, and not acted, He has never made a promise that He failed to bring to pass."

As a brief side note. the Holy Spirit has used verse 19 on more than one occasion to rescue me and deliver me. And as a result, by the grace of God, I've been able to spend time, thinking through and considering this verse carefully.

There are two thoughts worthy of our consideration, and they have the potential of becoming an anchor for you in your storm.

First, "God is not like man that he should lie," the idea here is that there is nothing about God that's like humanity—out of all the frailties you and I are vulnerable to, none of these exist within God.

Leviticus 17:11 states that the life of all flesh is in the blood. You and me are three-part beings (spirit, soul, and body) created by God to have fellowship with him. God is not opposed to humanity, it's just He's not a human being He is God. You and I, though we may not intend to, will lie.

Lying is associated with humanity, it is a human dynamic, and under the right situation, you and I will lie. This is true, and if you are in denial about this, even as you read this, that in itself is a form of lying...

The Scriptures declare that "it is impossible for God to lie." Some say that nothing is impossible with God. I say God cannot lie. I don't believe God could lie even if He tried. There is one, however, who was and is the father of all lying that is the devil.

Secondly, "nor the Son of Man that he would change his mind"

Though my understanding of the Hebrew language is limited, I'm fully persuaded by this phrase, "change His mind," in the Hebrew, I have found it to be both amazing and encouraging.

There is the sense here of "pressure," in other words, you and I can be under pressure from a situation or an event, either good or bad; and as a result, we may have to change our plans or make an adjustment—I will be forced to change my mind.

Beloved, there is no situation, event, or scenario that can pressure God into changing his mind, regarding any promise made to you and me. Now this is a good place for hallelujah!

This verse clearly says that God is not subject to the frailties of flesh and blood because God's origin is not from Adams seed.

Frailties, such as being flexible and responsive to outside pressures and conditions are nonexistent in regard to God's faithfulness to you and me.

Isaiah 46:9–10 says, "remember the former things, those of long ago; I am God, and there is no other; I am God, and there is none like me. I make known the end from the beginning, from ancient times, what is still to come. I say, 'my purpose will stand, and I will do all that I please.'"

We've already discussed God's wholeness and His perfection. We've come to understand that because He is perfect, there are no adjustments necessary. God does not have to be flexible, adaptable, or tentative in His actions toward you and me.

With that being said, He is never insensitive or harsh toward us and because His plans are perfect as well, every purpose, word, or course of action God is presently engaged or has already establish cannot be adjusted to accommodate some dynamic in our lives.

Secondly, He will never leave us. We are never forsaken, abandoned, or left without assistance in any circumstance that we face. Even the ones we are presently facing or have been facing for an extended period. (years) By applying this truth, mixing it with faith, and patience, it will bring about the demonstration of God's kingdom on your behalf, and you will be exposed to His "peace which surpasses all human understanding."

This is true whether I believe it or not, but the benefits, impact, and power of this truth is activated and experienced only as I in humility combine it with faith.

Considering this, think about God's original purpose and plan for man. With God already knowing the end from the very beginning, Adam's sin and Satan's operation were already factored into God's planning. God has not had to make any adjustments because of Satan, Adam, you, or me. Our successes and or failures do not affect the planning or timing the father has set in motion.

The Scriptures make it very clear that even Jesus being God's redemptive lamb, was determined "even before the foundation of the world." **(1 Pet. 1:20)**. That means before the creation of the heavens and the earth, i.e.—this physical natural universe—"God, who knows the end from the beginning" **(Isa. 46;10)** foresaw every forth coming incident—including the satanic rebellion in heaven, the fall of Adam, you and me, even to the very hour of Christ's return. In every incident, access to His kingdom's power is made available to all in and through faith in His son, Jesus, as a constant function. In algebraic math, a "constant function" is a function that has the same output value no matter what your input value is. This constancy is available for you and me for "whoever calls upon the name of the Lord shall be delivered."

Okay, okay, Pastor Ken, I get your point; but, Pastor, how do I apply this truth to your original proposition of living free from sin? And is that still a possibility?

==

So, let's revisit what I believe to be our foundational position.

Key

===

> If we are free from the root, sin the noun (hamartia),
> then we are also free from the fruit sin the verb (Hamartano).

So, every sinful behavior should be withering with the eventuality of ceasing to have its routine expression through us.

Harmatano, the verb form of the word sin, is generally defined in this manner to miss the mark, to miss the target, to miss the standard established by God, and to deviate from God's goal and not share in the prize.

Please note it's behaviorally based, your actions, acting in a way unlike God. This is how most define and determine whether they have sinned. And by the way, I am not suggesting that bad behavior is not sin, my intention is not in determining whether or not bad behavior is sinful, but in determining whether you and I can live free from sinful actions, expressions, and behaviors—(Harmatano) sin the verb.

Let's look again at the definition of the noun form of the word, "sin."

Hamartia, being born in a perpetual state of opposition to "God's Righteousness," originated from Adam's sin. This is a crucial key for understanding the application. Let's take a moment and chew on the noun form of the word, "sin," and see if we cannot extract some revelatory juices from it.

So, the first part of the definition is that of one being born we know that you and I were born in and under the authority Adam's sin. Because in our first birth, we were "born in a perpetual state of opposition to God and his righteousness which originated from Adam's sin."

Therefore, it is necessary for everyone to be born a second time—born again.

> Most surely, I say to you, unless one is born again, he cannot see the kingdom of God. (**John 3:3 NKJV**)

> Therefore, if anyone is in Christ, he is a new creation; old things have passed away; behold all things have become new. (**2 Corinthians 5:17**)

> "for I am not ashamed of the gospel of Christ, for it is the power of God to salvation for everyone who believes, for the Jew first and also for the Greek, for in it (the gospel) the righteousness of God is revealed from faith to faith i.e. (starting with faith, continuing by the same faith and ending by faith) as it is written, "the just shall live by faith" (**Romans 1:16–17**)

So, everything that we say and do in regard to experiencing freedom in Christ Jesus is by faith. You and I must be prepared to continue believing in the face of clear contradictions.

We have already established previously that Jesus is the root, you and I are the branches, the father is the gardener or the husband-man, and that the branch is the showcase for displaying the fruit produced from the root.

> I am the true vine (Root) and my Father is the vine dresser.
>
> Every branch in Me (that's you and me as new creations in Christ Jesus) that does not bear fruit He takes away and every branch that bears fruit He prunes that it may bear more fruit abide in Me and I in you as the branch cannot bear fruit of itself unless it abides in the vine, neither can you unless you abide in Me. **(John 15 1–4)**

But if a branch is severed from the root for any reason or for any period of time, it has an impact on the fruit—it begins to wither, become weakened, dried up, and will die.

Matthew 3:10 says, "And even now (Now is always now)." The axe is laid to the root of the trees; therefore, every tree (more than one kind of tree), which does not bear good fruit, is cut down and thrown into the fire.

I believe this verse contains a biblical principle, having more than one metaphorical and or contextual application. Therefore, consider this everything regarding the redemptive work of Jesus Christ on the cross. This is God the Father setting His Holy axe to the root of the tree, namely original sin noun (hamartia)," originating from Adam.

Key

==

> Anything in any dimension, physical or spiritual, should it become separated from its root, begins to be weakened. Secondly, if it should remain separated for an extended period, it will die—cease to exist—because it is cut off from its source of life and cannot continue to receive the strength it requires to produce and display its fruit.

Hebrews 10:5 says, "Therefore when Christ came into the world, He said: Sacrifice and offerings you (God the Father) did not desire, for a body thou has prepared for me."

Jesus, through the offering of this same body, which also contained five quarters of His sinless blood, has severed all of humanity from the "tree of the knowledge of good and evil" especially those who have believed. "The axe has been laid to the Root of the tree"— Adam's sin.

Hebrews 10:10 says, "And by that will, we have been made Holy through the sacrifice of the body of Jesus Christ, once for all time."

Because of God's love and mercy, we are enabled to engage this severance and all of its implications through the exercise of the measure of faith He has provided by which we are to maintain the severance through that same initial process.

Colossians 1:23a says, "If you continue in your faith, established and firm, and do not be moved from the hope held out in the gospel."

But just for a moment, I'd like for us to glimpse this process I believe to be depicted in old testament episodes of Israel's history.

Israel—God's chosen people and having been exposed on several occasions to "I am that I am"—understood that His attributes were revealed by the various names He chose to identify Himself with to Israel. There are at least ten recognized names that God used to revealed Himself and His character to Israel.

Every one of Israel's national and or individual needs were covered by the revelations of one or more of these names. Even the maintenance, provision, and health of their animals, all covered.

My immediate point is this everything touching the lives of God's people (Israel) was and is presently (you and me, provided for in abundance, "good measure, pressed down, shaken together and running over."

God engaged His people through constant and dramatic physical demonstrations of power and wisdom. Imagine all this functioned under an old and inadequate covenant, one that was never intended to be the final solution for the redemption of humanity.

So, beloved, ask yourself, "How much greater and more effective is God's provisions for every aspect of your life under the New Covenant signed in the holy blood of Jesus?"

Consider carefully the language used in this portion of Scripture.

> They (all the requirements of the old covenant) serve as a copy and shadow of the heavenly sanctuary. That is why Moses was warned when he was about to build the tabernacle, "see to it that you make everything according to the pattern shown you on the mountain now, however, Jesus has received a much more excellent ministry, just as the covenant he mediates is better, and is founded on better promises.

> For if that first covenant (the old covenant) had been without fault, no place would have been sought for a second.

> But God found fault with the people and said: "behold, the days are coming, declares the Lord, when I will make a new covenant with the house of Israel and with the house of Judah.

> It will not be like the covenant(the old covenant) I made with their fathers when I took them by the hand to lead them out of the land of Egypt, because they did not (and could not) abide by my covenant, and I disregarded them, declares the Lord.

> For this is the covenant I will make with the
> house of Israel after those days, declares the Lord. I
> will put my laws in their minds and write them on
> their hearts. And I will be their God, and they will
> be my people. **(Hebrews 8: 5–10)**

So, the first covenant God established, though perfect, proved to be ineffective because God's people were unable to meet the standard. Whether we aware of it or not, it was never God's intention or expectation for the law and the commandments to be met or kept. Now I know by making this statement many people may want to burn this book, but please, brethren, grant me one more second of your attention, considering this.

God's laws and commandments are perfect, they require a perfect response, but unfortunately there is only one human who's been able to respond perfectly to every law and commandment of God—that's the person of Jesus Christ. That's why He is the redeemer and not you, me, or anyone else.

The Bible says he did not come to put an end to the law and the commandments, but to fully complete them. With that said, no matter how hard Israel tried and, on many occasions, they really did try, they were never able to meet God's required standard, perfection.

In the books of Romans and Galatians, there are several portions of scripture, which in my opinion, clearly defined God's purpose and reasonings for the law and the commandments.

In twenty-five words or less, it says this to demonstrate the futility in man's attempt at meeting God's standard of righteousness because humanity is born infected by sin the noun (hamartia, originating from Adam's sin).

We can never rise to the level of God's wholeness. Secondly and as important, the law and the commandments were given to exacerbate man's failure, acting as a schoolmaster, by converting this experience into a revelation of how deeply they needed "God's Lamb" Jesus Christ, the only deliverer, redeemer, and savior.

As I said earlier, I'd like for us to glimpse God's process for complete freedom. I believe to be depicted in this old testament episode in Israel's history.

The Bronze Serpent

Israel had been wandering for almost forty years in this wilderness setting, and though seemingly isolated in this environment, their bodies didn't get sick, their clothing didn't wear out, and they had more than enough food and water.

As a matter of fact, they were being provided supernaturally with many of their needs, literally falling from the sky. They experienced the daily presence of the Lord, and yet Adam's sin dominated their lives.

==

So, Aaron has recently died, his priesthood was stripped from him and placed upon his son, Eleazer. The people mourned for thirty days over the loss of Aaron, and as they move toward the south, a Canaanite king heard Israel was coming. He promptly set himself to waged war against them, and he took some of them as prisoners. Israel makes a deal or vow to the Lord: vowing that if He would deliver their brethren from this king and his people into their hands, they would utterly destroy everything about them.

NUMBERS 21:3 (NKJV)

> And the Lord listen to the voice of Israel and delivered up the Canaanites, and the utterly destroyed them, and their cities and so the name of that place was called hormah" then they journeyed from Mount Hor by the way of the Red Sea, to go around the land of Edom; and the soul of the people became very discouraged on the way.

And the people spoke against God and against Moses: "why have you brought us up out of Egypt to die in the wilderness? For there is no food and no water, and our soul loathes this worthless bread"

So the Lord sent fiery serpents among the people, and they bit the people; and many of the people of Israel died.

Therefore, the people came to Moses, and said, "we have sinned, and we have spoken against the Lord and against you; pray to the Lord that He take away the serpents from us." So, Moses prayed for the people.

Then the Lord said to Moses, "make a fiery serpent, and set it on a pole; and it shall be that everyone who is bitten, when he looks at it, shall live."

So Moses made a bronze serpent, and put it on a pole; and so it was if the serpent had bitten anyone, whenever he looked at the bronze serpent he lived. (**Numbers 21:4-9 NKJV**)

There are several potent points to be considered in this text, but with your permission, I would to highlight only a few so that we can make an application as to how you and I can consistently live in the place of freedom from sin that God has called us to live.

Verse 4 says, "And the soul of the people became very discouraged along the way."

This is a very important point on any occasion when you, as a believer, are attacked and targeted by the enemy. I'm referring to new covenant believers. The point of this attack will always occur within the confines of the soul first. Now, as a quick review, the soul is comprised of the mind (the way that you think), the emotions (the way you feel), and your will (your capacity to make a choice i.e. decision-making).

The single most effective mechanism in the arsenal of satanic weaponry is his capacity to manage the physical natural realm.

Therefore, he wants all of our decisions, choices, and the actions we take to be resulting from the things we see, the things we feel, and the way we think.

Our souls are created by God to instinctively function within the construct of this physical/natural environment. The soul is created to assess all physical information, to conclude its meaning, to calculate, and make determinations.

So, most of the information we are exposed to, especially when it comes to our life in Christ or the things that God has for us, is within an environment of the lie. It has been manipulated so that should we respond to it, it would net our destruction.

This is why there are countless instructions throughout the Scripture that encourage us not to war, live, or pursue a life framed by our own understanding consider these next verses

> Trust in the Lord with all your heart, (your spirit) and do not lean on your own understanding; in all your ways acknowledge him and he shall direct your path i.e. choose to allow the

Holy Spirit and or the word of God to have authority over your own opinions and ideas. Do not be wise in your own eyes; fear the Lord and depart from evil. **(Proverbs 3:5–7)**

While we do not look at the things which are seen, but at the things which are not seen. For the things which are seen are temporary, but the things which are not seen are eternal. **(2 Corinthians 4:18)**

These are just a couple of verses, and I'm sure you can think of several immediately on your own. But the primary point here is for us to glimpse the arena in which the enemy will always try and draw us into, so that he can manage us in that environment.

What is it that makes us so vulnerable to being drawn into this arena? Well, as I've stated in a previous portion of this book, it is our own personal pride and our propensity for wanting to make the decision ourselves and be just like God. Beware, brethren, love and humility are your only source of deliverance and protection from this most appealing place.

Verse 5 says, "Whenever we surrender to the pressure and lure of our souls, they force our mouth to declare bitterness, frustration, unbelief and fear; notice Israel immediately they began to complain."

First about the person God has set as the leader, and secondly about God himself. Today, on many occasions, people tend to direct their complaints about the pastor or the person leading—why did they do it like this, why don't they just do that, or we should do it a different way. Or perhaps you've heard them complain about God (if God really loved me, this is what would happen). Why is God taking so long? I don't understand what God is doing. I'm mad at God.

At the root of most complaints are two basic things—fear and unbelief. Israel expressed their fear with these statements on why have you brought us into the wilderness? to die? (that was their fear talking).

Secondly, with unbelief, there is no food or water—they did not believe that God was able to continue providing for them, or that God's provisions though supernatural, would continue, as they were sick and tired of the same thing.

In verse 6, this behavior opens the door for fiery serpents—judgments and curses—that now have access to us. Always remember this, the snakes and wild animals, whose natural habitat was the wilderness, was not a problem for Israel. Those things always existed, but God kept them at bay by being a shield about his people.

But on more than one occasion, when Israel sins, God lifts his protection; and outside forces invaded the camp. Likewise, on this occasion, this must've been extraordinarily terrifying for the approximately two million people.

Living in this community, to put it in perspective, I live outside of Boston where there are approximately two million people in the entire city. I can just imagine if twenty thousand people during the course of a day suddenly died.

Not only that, but the manner in which they died poisonous snakes just suddenly invaded the city and fatally bit twenty thousand people. I believe there would be a terror throughout the city of Boston that no one would ever forget.

So, we can see here that the fiery serpents are a picture of Satan, and the venom a picture of the potency of sin being injected into humanity's bloodstream, producing horrific death.

Now, this terror as you can see (a) serves a purpose of bringing people to the point of repentance and then secondly it opens the door for God's redemptive process.

So, let's see the keys found in God's solution. The fiery serpent was supposed to be taken by Moses and placed upon a pole. The people simply had to look toward it, and even though they were bitten with an incurable disease, they could still be delivered.

The serpent in my opinion is a picture of Jesus Christ on the cross, only after being on the cross is Jesus view as undesirable, like the ugly serpent.

Only because now, He has taken upon Himself all of the poison of your sin and certainly all of mine. When on the cross, Jesus is not depicted as beautiful. As a matter fact, **Isaiah 53**, a prophetic chapter about the Savior, says this, "He has no form or comeliness that we find attractive and, when we see him there is no beauty that we should desire him. it goes on to say, that we hid as it were our faces from him" and that the ripping out of his beard made him almost unrecognizable as human."

Jesus, representing the curse, "cursed is everyone the Scripture says who hangs on a tree" **(Galatians 3:13 NKJV)**.

Secondly, the pole represented the cross at Calvary. Remember when Israel first left Egypt, the Bible says that a mixed multitude came out with them, in other words, not everyone of the approximately two and a half-million people that left Egypt on that miraculous night were all Jews. I believe that people from Africa, Egypt, and other surrounding cities, and countries, were all part of the Exodus.

So, now, God says to Moses whoever would look to the current serpent on the cross and here's the key keep his focus on him that person would live even though they were bitten. Now, just a quick observation, the word that's used here in Hebrew for the word, "live," is a very interesting word. It is the verb, "Raah," it has this simple definition, its causative—in other words, anyone holding his gaze upon the serpent on the pole,—(Jesus on the Cross)—would recover from his bite, (the resurrection).

I would like to take just few moments and point us into a slightly different direction. Please allow this detour to act as a warning for us and especially those of us who have a broader and deeper base of biblical knowledge. The apostle, Paul, said in 1 Corinthians 8:. that knowledge tends to puff one up. So, to all of us, be careful.

Here are two brief episodes on our detour that are worth embracing and prayerfully taking your own pulse as we continue.

First, almost every time throughout Israel's history, whenever God did something dramatic, using a physical manifestation, the people tended to become idolatrous as a result of this extraordinary event—the bronze serpent, after the judgment of God allowing fiery serpents entry into the camp, the ones who gazed upon the "bronze serpent" on the pole were healed and delivered from such a traumatic and deathly experience. Initially, the people retained a healthy relationship with God's instrument of deliverance.

However, after a season of familiarity, a commonness consumed the people, the bronze serpent literally lost its power.

I don't believe it was because God's anointing was lifted. I believe it had everything to do with the people's familiarity with the supernatural. For almost seven hundred years after this event, the people kept as sacred the bronze serpent. It became a part of Israel's heathenistic worship practice, in the high places, it was finally destroyed by King Hezekiah.

In **2.Kings 18: 4**, it says that young King Hezekiah was twenty-five years old when he began to reign, and that he did what was right in the eyes of the Lord.)He removed the high places, smash the sacred stones, and cut down the assurah polls. He broke into pieces the bronze snake Moses had made. Up to that time, the Israelites had been burning incense to it, and they called it *nehushtan*.

This object, having been constructed and designed by God for the purpose of Israel to gaze upon, now had lost its purpose and its divine function. This object and Israel's relationship to it had a form of godliness but was indeed denying the very power thereof.

Our second example is when the Philistines captured the ark of the covenant. Israel went out to fight against the Philistines as Israel was fighting the Philistines defeated them and killed 4000 men on the battlefield.

When the survivors returned, they were stunned and wondered why God had brought defeat on them that day. They thought it was because they didn't bring the ark of the covenant with them. So, they decided to bring the ark of the covenant from Shiloh—its sacred place—so that the ark may go with us and save us from the hand of our enemies. And so, they brought the ark to the battlefield. Scripture says that when the ark entered Israel's camp, there was such an uproar, such a shout made by Israel, that the ground shook, and the Philistines were initially shaken by this turn of events.

They said we are doomed, who will deliver us from the hand of the mighty God of Israel. Then the Philistines encouraged each other to be strong, to hold their ground, and to fight.

So, they fought the Israelites, and on that day, thirty thousand Israelites were defeated. Every man fled to his tent, the slaughter was very great, Israel also lost the ark of God, it was captured and even the two sons of Eli, Hophni and Phineas, were killed.

Now there are other examples, but we're going to limit this detour to just these two. So, what's your point, Pastor Ken? My point is this sometimes our familiarity with biblical principles, in the process of experiencing victory in Christ Jesus, can become so matter of fact that the freshness, the potency, and the dynamic of power available to each and every one is only experienced by those who, in humility keep their attitudes, and their mindsets fresh and tender to the things of God.

We should not be allowing, callousness, arrogance, presumptions or knowledge, about the things of God to choke off God's presence in you.

Key

==

> Believing and receiving is faith's two-step process, but it is through faith and patience this is how we inherit the promises of God.

God has set himself to function within the framework of time. What I mean is that even in creation, He took six days. He established the process of beginning and ending, which implies time. This is why patience is absolutely essential. Faith functions within the context of patience, and faith cannot develop outside of one being patient. There is what I refer to as "creative time." This is the invisible period starting after God has spoken and ending when the promise comes to pass. There is usually a period of time between that occasion.

That space of time is the environment in which your faith and your patience develops producing maturity and wholeness inside of you and me.

Looking a little further into the exercise of faith and patience as essential components in the application process, let's take a brief look at. **James 1:1–8 (NIV)**:

James a bondservant of God and of the Lord Jesus Christ, to the 12 tribes which are scattered abroad greetings consider it pure joy, my brothers, whenever you face trials of many kinds, because you know that the testing of your faith, develops perseverance. Perseverance must finish its work so that you may be mature and complete, not lacking anything.

If any of you lacks wisdom, he should ask God, who gives generously to all without finding fault, and it will be given to him.

But when he asked, he must believe and not doubt, because he who doubts is like a wave of the sea, blown and tossed by the wind.

That man should not think he will receive a anything from the Lord;

He is a double-minded man, unstable in all he does.

Let's take a moment and set this text in a context so that we get a clearer sense of how to apply the principles here effectively. First, we can see that the letter was written to the twelve tribes—newly born-again messianic Jews. The implication here is that persecution was going on, and believers everywhere were being severely harassed, and persecuted, being driven in all directions out of Jerusalem. This is James, not the apostle, but Jesus's brother.

He is writing these words to encourage, inspire, and strengthen those who no doubt are experiencing a sense of abandonment, helplessness, fear, and frustration—"oh, Lord, where are you, please help." I am sure that on more than one occasion, you have felt like this yourself, maybe your reasonings for reading this book is your way of saying, "Lord I need your help."

Notice the first thing that James identifies in this process of application is attitude. Consider it pure joy, brethren, on most occasions whenever we are being challenged. We are not thinking of it as a joyful occasion.

So, first, there needs to be a change in my attitude. This is easily accomplished when I remember and truly understand "that" the battle is not mine, but the battle is the Lord.

> King Jehoshaphat was facing a vast army, he declared "Lord we do not know what to do, but our eyes are on you" the Lord reminds King Jehoshaphat with these words
>
> Listen King Jehoshaphat, and all who live in Judah and Jerusalem (and all who live in your house and your family) this is what the Lord says to you: do not be afraid or discouraged because of this vast army. For the battle is not yours, but the Lords.
>
> You will not have to fight this battle take your position (your position of faith and

patience) and stand firm, and you will see the deliverance of the Lord only do not be afraid; do not be discouraged, the Lord will be with you. **(2 Chronicles 20:15, 17)**

When you face any trial, remembering and understanding this, you will be supernaturally enabled to stand your ground with a sense of joy and confidence in the faithfulness of God.

Key

==

> Please remember…everything about the kingdom of God is "on earth as it is in heaven." It already is, so it is not by might, me trying or my efforts, but by the work of the Holy Spirit and me entering into God's rest.

As a side note, you'll notice that there is an expectation in the text that we are not avoiding trials, the operative word is when you face trials.

There is something the writer presumes the readers already knows that is this. God's interacting with you and me is not supposed to be some fluffy Disneyland type experience or some kind of fairytale with a fuzzy bearded character.

"He who began the work in you is continuing faithfully that work until it is fully complete" (**Philippians 1:6 NIV**). So, the work He has begun in us is the development of His person and character inside of His people.

This is a lifetime project and the first thing being developed is perseverance—a determination never to give up and to always stand your ground, demonstrating God's faithfulness to a lost world.

You and I must allow this process—perseverance—to finish its work in us. Like some fruit, you must wait for it to be fully mature before it can be consumed. If this process is allowed to complete its function, then you and I will become full and complete, lacking nothing.

We become people that God can entrust with different assignments in His kingdom, being a fully matured representative and ambassador for and in Christ Jesus.

I can almost hear the voice of the Lord speaking about you, saying, "Well done, my good and faithful servant"

This is not a complicated process. If you are uncertain, lack divine wisdom in grasping the application, or the implementation of this principle, just asked the Father. He will provide the wisdom for you, and He won't poke fun of you, think less of you or find fault with you.

So, here, I'll share some wisdom regarding faith and receiving. The text says, "When you ask you must believe and not doubt, because he who doubts is like a wave of the sea blown and tossed by the wind, that man should not think he will receive, anything from the Lord." Everything about God and His kingdom is designed like this, "every good and perfect gift comes down from the father of lights."

Everything that's good and perfect is coming from God. God is the giver. So, If God is the giver, how does what he gives get into the hands of those he's giving it to?

Simple answer, it must be received, accepted. Someone asked me, "Pastor Ken, how do you receive?" I have found this to be a legitimate question, and on more than one occasion, it has been demonstrated to me that many of us do not understand how to receive.

The word receive in the new covenant is the Greek word, "Lambano." It means this to take, to take hold with your hand, to lay hold of, and what I found to be a very helpful idea is this "to take possession of, to take ownership of by making it your own and never letting it go.

I have found that if someone gives you something, and you really believe it's yours, you take possession of it. You don't give it back, you begin to think about how it's going to serve you because it's yours, and you believe that.

But on the contrary, if you take possession of something, but you really don't believe it yours, you relate to it very tentatively, and if someone said, "I'm sorry, could you return that to me," you are more than likely going to be willing to give it back. By the way, this strategy of returning and giving back is another tactic in which the thief steals from you and me.

God's process is giving, believing, and receiving. "Thank you, Lord, for giving to me. I receive it because I trust your faithfulness that you have given it."

So, when the Lord is saying that the man who doesn't believe cannot receive anything from the Lord, God is not saying, "Well if you don't believe me, I'm not giving you anything," in some kind of punitive manner.

What's being shared here is this, the importance of receiving. Because unless you are able to receive, take possession without giving it back, you will be blown and tossed about by the wind.

You accepted it, and then you'll give it back, you'll say "I have it," then, "I thought I had it." You'll say, "Yes, I am sure," then you'll say, "I'm not sure. Tossed about like a wave of the sea."

So, we can see how a double-minded man is unstable in all he does. If he has never made his own, that which is to be received from the Lord, he becomes vulnerable to having it taken from him.

There are two words here that represent the term, "double-minded," one is the word, "dipsychos," and the second is "Schizo," meaning two-souled—two sets of thoughts functioning at the same time. It's where we get the word, "schizophrenia," a hellish and torturous mental issue.

It's not as though God is holding something back because His kingdom is designed to be received by faith, so we will need to take possession and make our own everything the father has for us.

But remember, it's through faith and patience is how we inherit God's promises. Consider **Mark 4: 26–28**:

> He also said, this is what the kingdom of God is like. A man scatter seed on the ground.
>
> Night and day, whether he sleeps or gets up, the seed sprouts and grows, though he does not know how.
>
> All by itself the soil produces grain-first the stock, then the head, then the full kernel in the head.

And so now, hopefully, we can clearly see that all the promises in the kingdom of God are all ours. So beloved remember in His invisible, heavenly dimension, everything is fully accomplished and presently available.

But in this physical, natural realm, we are exercising faith and patience because these things are developmental in this realm. Because time is of the fabric and function of this physical dimension.

It is truly finished, and as we stand our ground in this truth, you and I will see the salvation of the Lord in every regard.

The same principle and process we are to apply to being delivered from the root and being free from the fruit of sin.

Let's consider one more Scriptural episode

The next day as they were leaving Bethany, Jesus was hungry.

seeing in the distance a fig tree in leaf, he went to find out if it had any fruit. When he reached it, he found nothing but leaves, because it was not the season for figs.

Then He said to the tree, "may no one ever eat fruit from you again." And His disciples heard Him say it.

In the morning, as they went along, they saw the fig tree withered from the roots. Peter remembered and said to Jesus, "Rabbi, look! The fig tree you cursed has withered!"

Have faith in God, Jesus answered.

Truly I tell you, if anyone says to this mountain, go, throw yourself into the sea, and does not doubt in their heart but believes that what they say will happen, it will be done for them.

Therefore, I tell you, whatever you ask for in prayer, believe that you have received it, and it will be yours.

And when you stand praying, if you hold anything against anyone, forgive them so that your Father in heaven may forgive you Your sins. **(Mark 11:12–25(NIV)**

==

First of all, there is an abundance of clear and remarkable exposition on this portion of Scripture. My only purpose and position on this occasion is in observing this principle of freedom from the root equals freedom from the fruit. So, there will be several points that I will not address.

Hebrews 4:14–16 is a very a comforting verse of Scripture. It clearly connects us to Jesus in terms of purpose and motives, regarding His desire for fellowship with you and me, it says:

> Since we have a great high priest who has gone through the heavens, Jesus the son of God. Let us hold firmly to the faith we profess.
>
> Because Jesus is not the kind of high priest, who is unable to sympathize or relate with our weaknesses. But He is one who has been tempted in every way just as we are, yet without sin.
>
> Because this is the case we can come with boldness unto the throne of grace and with confidence, so that we may receive mercy and find grace to help us in our time of need.

There is a common theme in these two portions of Scripture, which at times can be slightly hidden. But now I believe is made visible from the heart of God by the Holy Spirit. It is this, Jesus came and lived as a real man—a human being, one born as a baby. He cried, needed to be cared for, had earthly parents, and for thirty-three and a half years, set himself to live within the limitations of this physical life, while at the same time, fulfilling God's purpose for His life and then, he died.

So, everything about Jesus says to you and me I know what you mean. I know what you fee, and what your challenges are because I have gone through an experienced everything you do. I know even more fully than you, the size, the construct, and the enormous power and framework of your every challenge.

I have provided for you an instrument for conquest, so rest assured that no weapon in your life, which sets itself against you, will prosper, for I have already conquered all of Satan's contradictions and oppositions against you and the Father's purpose in you.

This is the covenant that I've made with you and I signed the bottom line in my own blood. Signed, Jesus your brother, your high priest, your savior, Lord, and king

Now, let's consider **Mark 11:12**—And one of the first things we glimpse here is Jesus's humanity.

He, with his disciples, having spent the night in Bethany, probably with his close friends, Mary, Martha, and Lazarus, is now on his way back to the temple in Jerusalem. It's early morning and breakfast time, and he's hungry just like you and me.

And seeing alongside the road a fig tree in leaf, the fact that it had leaves on it, was an indication that there was the possibility of fruit being present as well, edible fruit that is. So, he goes over for a closer investigation, and when he reached it, he found nothing but leaves because it was not the full season for figs.

Jesus is not being impulsive nor is he acting out of frustration by deciding to use his ability as punishment to a tree for not satisfying him. On the contrary, Jesus always uses every encounter, and any episode in life, as a point of instruction for his people—you and me.

So, He Speaks to the tree "may no one ever eat fruit from you again." I want us to view this language as God's axe being laid to the root of this tree.

We've already established that fruit is the product of the root, so when Jesus is speaking, His speech is directed to the root. His speech and His focus are not on the visible part. The leaves, the branches, or the fruit that should've been on the tree but to the part, which is not seen, the hidden.

He's addressing the root. Now when the root is affected, or severed from its purpose, in this case, "no more producing any fruit."

When no more figs can be produced on this tree, the tree has no further reason to exist. Notice the disciples heard Him. Jesus is revealing a significant spiritual principle here.

They spend the night in Jerusalem, overturning the tables of the money changers in the temple, fulfilling even more biblical prophecy, and declaring my house shall be a house of prayer, but you've made it a den of thieves.

Now, the next morning, they are following the same route as the day before. And now, they physically see the fig tree withered from the roots.

Peter remembers hearing Jesus speak to it, says, "Rabbi look! The fig tree you cursed has withered!"

Jesus's response is with God's foundational key to everything—"have faith in God." One Greek translation of this phrase is this, "Have the God kind of faith."

Think about that for a moment, can you have "God's kind of faith?" If you are a believer, that's exactly what's resident inside of you. Scripture says that God in his wisdom "has given to every man the measure/a measure of his own faith." We have within us the capacity to "trust the Lord with all of our hearts and not depend upon our own understanding."

Throughout the gospels, there is a comment that Jesus makes on more than one occasion, it is this "oh ye of little faith" for a time, I perhaps like you, was under the impression that Jesus was referring to the amount of faith that a person has. But upon a more careful review of the language I now realize, He was not referring to a small or great amount of faith.

This is why he makes this statement in another place in the gospel, saying, "If you have faith the size of a grain of mustard seed, you could say to this mountain be removed from here and be cast into the sea."

I believe Jesus to be referring to the black mustard seed—a seed widespread in that general terrain and commonly used in that culture. It was indeed the smallest seed in that region.

The word used for "little faith" is the Greek word, *oglio-pistis*. It's language that has more to do with exercise and development than an amount or size of something.

E.G. a muscle. The more you exercise it, the more reliable it is in its ability to produce service for you. The opposite is true as well, the less exercise, the less serviceable your God kind of faith.

He continues to show the dynamics of this principle, He says, "I'll tell you the truth, if anyone, (by the way you are and anyone). Says to this mountain, Whatever problem you might have no matter how big or small it might be go throw yourself into the sea and does not doubt in his heart but believes what he says will happen it will be done for him."

Because this is the case, I will tell you whatever you ask for in prayer, believe that you have received it, and it will be yours. Receiving anything from the Lord has everything to do with having it before you see it because everything in the invisible realm is presently available. And it will be yours, and notice this promise is future tense.

So, here again, we see a picture of an axe being laid to the root of a tree. Spiritually, when struck, it dies instantaneously, just like Adam the day he ate the fruit. He was instantly separated from God, i.e.—spiritual death—but physically, his death was not demonstrated until his 962nd birthday.

So, likewise, as you and me in faith declare our freedom from the root, we are instantly released from the authority of Adam's sin. And as we continually stand our ground in this matter, we will see the withering and ceasing to exist many and ugly habit.

And then He reiterates this principle again in what I believe to be divine clarity, "Therefore, I tell you, whatever you ask for, believe that you have received it, and it will be yours."

As an addendum to this verse, I always like to add **1 John 5:14–15**, "Remember it's only truth that sets us free and this is the confidence that we have in him, if we ask anything, according to his will, he hears us, and if we know that he hears us, whatsoever we desired from him, we will have it."

So, we get a clear sense here that as long as we are praying and exercising the "God kind of faith" within the construct and the contexts of God's purpose and plan for our lives. it is then that "no weapon that moves against us, that tries to interfere with us, will know success."

Therefore, by the power of the Holy Spirit, we can move forward, derailing any opposition of the enemy. This is a good place for hallelujah!!

And lastly, we get to see also that no matter the dynamic, everything flows, everything is released from and through God's focal point of forgiveness. "Forgive so that your Father in Heaven may forgive you, your sins."

Our forgiveness is how we access His forgiveness. Remember, as we have begun in faith, we are to continue in that same faith "the just shall continually day in and day out, live in a manner in which they are trusting the Lord every day"

===

Should we fail to continually exercise faith in the context of having been delivered from the root, then the same roots can begin to restore themselves, and if not corrected, the same tree will be restored, beware brethren, root fruit can be restored.

But the continual exercise of faith keeps the head of the axe applied to the root of the tree, allowing the root fruit to be in a perpetual state of withering and eventual death. Your experience with some of your horrific struggles, those things will begin to be diminished in and through your personality.

But if anyone fails to continually trust the original work of God's redemptive process an began to rely upon his or her own ability to manage their behavior, then consider this principle found in **Matthew 12:43–45 (NIV)**.

When an evil spirit comes out of a man, it goes through arid places seeking rest and does not find it.

Then it says, "I will return to the house I left." When it arrives, it finds the house unoccupied, swept, and put in order.

Then it goes and takes with it seven other spirits more wicked than itself, and they go in and live there. And the final condition of that man is worse than the first. This is how will be with this wicked generation.

I am fully aware of the spiritual and biblical context of this portion of Scripture and its application to a demonic entity. But with that said, I want us to consider the "hidden principle" in the context of our discussion. Let's review this one more time

The axe is laid to the root of the tree the root is the noun— every evil behavior associated with Adam's sin because Jesus always delivers from the root. You and I, through faith in Jesus Christ, have been delivered. Our lives are severed from sin the noun. The verb is merely a side effect of the noun. The verb has no legal standing and technically no place to draw strength and function from. But this is only true as we maintain our connection through the continued exercise of faith.

Have you ever cut a tree flat to the ground, under certain situations that tree will begin to grow again? Olive trees are notorious for this process, as well as many other kinds of trees, because everything springs from the root.

After a tree is severed from its root, the fruit eventually dies. As long as the root is kept separated from the tree, the process of death continues until complete annihilation.

Leviticus 17:11 says, "The life of the flesh is in the blood." Consider this example. Take a rubber band and place it around one of your fingers. Shortly, that finger can become numb because the connection to the root (blood) is being restricted and immediately a lack of sensation begins to be affected in that finger. If sustained long enough, that finger will literally be amputated and severed from your body.

Finally, you and I, through Jesus Christ, have been delivered from the root of sin that relates back to Adam. So, separation from the root must and can be maintained. This is accomplished as we persistently exercise our faith in this process—you and me, resting in and continuously trusting the finished work of Jesus.

So, in any situation, God's forgiveness of sin is always the solution to my problem. As you know, some types of fruit appear and are ready for harvest quicker than others, trees, plants, grass, etc.

This is why when you first received Jesus as your savior, some of your severe issues came to an abrupt halt, and overnight, they ceased to be a problem for you. Yet there are other areas in which, after all these years, you continue to struggle with. You've prayed and have had others pray for you, and yet these disappointing pockets seem to persist unabatedly.

Beloved, the evidence of death is experienced in varying degrees, nonetheless the moment the root is severed death is introduced. And sin the verb—all of your sinful behaviors—will eventually wither and cease to express themselves by your constancy in God's process.

This is vitally important!! Death and all of its side effects (bad behaviors) have no strength of its own, no legal authority to function, unless it extracts it from sin the noun—the root.

Key

==

> Truth is what God said, not what I think he said, truth is what God means, not what I think he means.

Lastly, brethren, please consider these final thoughts

As descendant from Adam, our common focus is always the visible first, the present, and the now. Most believers are consumed with their present behavior and actions. But true victory in Christ Jesus has everything to do with choosing the life of faith. It started in faith, it is maintained in that same faith, and will eventually end as a result of the original faith. This is what the text in **Hebrews 11:6 (NIV)** is saying, "And without faith it is impossible to please God, because anyone who comes to him must believe, that he exists and that he rewards those who earnestly seek him."

Unfortunately, when we mistakenly believe that good behavior is God's standard of righteousness, we are drawn into a carnal confrontation where my triumph is dependent upon my ability—human effort.

Whenever I observe my behavior to be unlike Jesus, I immediately began the process of self-management. As a result, my life with Christ is seasoned with constant failure, frustration, and re-dedications time and time again.

But when Jesus released, rescued, and restored us from the law of sin and death, faith in His "once for all time" act of redemption was the only requirement for a free indeed life.

Now, I will keep my focus on this truth, believing I was set free from Adams original sin, when I accepted Jesus Christ, as my redeemer and Savior.

And as I continually declare the authority of that event, as a once and all-time occurrence, I am a new creation. The old me has passed away, and a new me has come into existence. I became the righteousness of God. And through my continued faith in that historical event, I continue to be that same righteousness.

My only fight is the fight of faith in my connection to God and His kingdom through this simple truth. Then and only then will the contradictions of my everyday experiences. Be weakened first, then each began to cease to exist as they lose their ability to impose themselves in my life. This is a lifetime process "for He who began the work is the one who is faithfully continuing that same work unto full completion" **(Phil. 1:6 NIV)**.

I can indeed be holy as He is holy and demonstrate the righteousness of God by the power and person of the Holy Spirit living in and through me. If I am led by the spirit, I am not fulfilling the lust of my flesh, and if you are free from the root, you are free from the fruit.

Key

===

Consider, beloved, this last thought in the context of all that's been said.

1 John 1:7 (NKJV) says that if we walk in the light as He is in the light, we have fellowship with one another, and the blood of Jesus Christ, His Son cleanses us from all sin. (noun).

The word, "cleanse," is a present tense verb, and without much ado, it's simply saying this. At any time, you and I look unto Jesus, trusting Him as in the beginning, His sinless blood, even in that moment continually cleanses us and keep us as the righteousness of God.

So, likewise, as we continually trust God's process of deliverance from sin the root, then you and I can begin to live a life of freedom from Sin the fruit.

About the Author

Pastor Ken, as he is affectionately known, has pastored for about thirty years. He and his wife, Katie, have been married for forty-six years. They have four sons, one daughter, and at present, fourteen grandchildren.

Pastor Ken is well known through-out the city of Worcester and the surrounding towns of Massachusetts as a gifted and anointed Bible teacher and communicator. His careful instruction in Scripture is respected from the Island of Martha's Vineyard and throughout Cape Cod where he started and for several years pastored the New Kingdom Worship Center. His consistent message of "faith in the faithfulness, mercy and grace of God" is impacting the lives of many.